KNITS

May Gibbs KNITS

Designs by Kathy Jarvis,
Wyn McNamara and Sue Morton

PURE NEW WOOL

CLICK CLACK.
Cleckheaton

BayBooks
An imprint of HarperCollins*Publishers*

Contents

Introduction

May Gibbs was born Cecilia May Gibbs in Surrey, England in 1877. In 1881 she emigrated to Australia with her parents and brothers. As a child she was actively encouraged by her parents to draw. Her first book, *Snugglepot and Cuddlepie*, was published in 1918 and has never been out of print. May went on to create more wonderful stories and characters which have entertained children and adults alike ever since.

Still Australia's most well-loved children's author and illustrator, her friendly bush creatures and adorable flower babies have delighted generations of Australian children. Her drawings and designs have become popular icons of Australian culture and remain a symbol of the beauty and fragility of the Australian bush.

Copyright of all May Gibbs' work rests with the Spastic Centre of New South Wales and the New South Wales Society for Children and Young Adults with Physical Disabilities and royalties from the sale of this book benefit these two charities. The beautiful garments inspired by May Gibbs' illustrations and stories are intended for personal wear and not for any commercial purpose. They have been designed with the approval and co-operation of the copyright holders and their agent, Curtis Brown (Australia) Pty. Ltd.

Sizes and Measurements

Each pattern has a tabled list of measurements for easy reference. Make sure you measure your child or yourself before starting to knit. Note: Figures in brackets throughout the pattern refer to the larger sizes. Where only one number appears it applies to all sizes. If you are knitting a complicated pattern you may find it helpful to mark the directions for the size you are knitting with a highlighting pen.

Knitting Needles

Metric sizes are referred to throughout the pattern. English equivalents are given in the Materials section at the beginning of each pattern. Needles are available in different lengths. Always consider the size of the garment you are knitting before purchasing needles. Needles that are too short for the number of stitches required will make knitting difficult.

When knitting with a set of 4 double pointed needles, divide stitches equally over 3 needles and use remaining needle to knit stitches. Each needle is used in turn to knit off. If working with a large number of stitches, corks on the ends of each needle will prevent stitches being pushed off.

Tension

Each pattern has a tension chart. It is most important that you knit a tension square before starting any pattern, otherwise the measurements will be wrong and the finished garment may differ in appearance from the garment photographed. Tension for plain and textured patterns sometimes differs and it is necessary to knit two squares. If your square is smaller than specified you will need to use larger size needles. If your square is larger you will need to use smaller needles.

Abbreviations

cm = centimetres
in = inches
mm = millimetres
pr = pair
st/s = stitch/es
K = knit
P = purl
st st = stocking stitch (1 row K, 1 row P)
C4F = Slip next 4 sts onto a cable needle and leave at front of work, K4, then K4 from cable needle.
beg = beginning
inc = increase
dec = decrease
patt = pattern
foll = following
as folls = as follows
rep = repeat
rem = remaining
rib = (K1, P1) rep until end of row or for number of sts indicated
cont = continued
alt = alternate
tog = together
MC = main colour
C1 = first contrast colour
C2 = second contrast colour
C3 = third contrast colour, etc.
yfwd = yarn forward
yrn = yarn round needle
M1 = Pick up loop which lies before next stitch, place on left-hand needle and knit through back of loop.
tbl = through back of loop
Make Bobble = (K1, P1, K1, P1) all in next st, pass 2nd, 3rd and 4th sts over first to form a bobble.
ybk = yarn back
sl1 = slip one stitch: insert the right-hand needle into the next stitch on the left-hand needle as if to knit it. Slip the stitch off the needle onto the right-hand needle.
psso = pass the slipped stitch over: with the point of the left-hand needle, lift up the slipped stitch and pass it over the stitch just knitted and off the needle.
CR = Slip next st onto a cable needle and leave at back of work, K3, then K1 from cable needle
CL = Slip next 3 sts onto a cable needle and leave at back of work, K1, then K3 from cable needle.
CRP = Slip next st onto a cable needle and leave at front of work, K3, then P1 from cable needle.
CLP = Slip next 3 sts onto a cable needle and leave at front of work, P1, then K3 from cable needle.

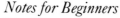

Notes for Beginners

The following instructions will help you with some of the basic skills and stitches needed to successfully complete the patterns in this book.

BASIC STITCHES

Knit stitch and purl stitch are the two basic knitting stitches. When every row is knitted back and forth on two needles, garter stitch is formed. When one row is knitted and the next purled, stocking stitch is formed. When working in the round, knitting every row produces stocking stitch. A combination of knit and purl stitches, usually one knit stitch and one purl stitch, in the same row, is known as ribbing. Ribbing is used on sleeve and body edges to form a neat, stretchable finish. It is usually worked on smaller needles than the body of the garment.

KNIT STITCH

1. With the yarn at the back, insert your right-hand needle from front to back into the 1st stitch on your left-hand needle.
2. Bring your working yarn under and over the point of your right-hand needle.
3. Draw a loop through and slide the 1st stitch off your left-hand needle while the new stitch is retained on your right-hand needle. Continue in this way to the end of the row.
4. To knit the next row, turn the work around so that the back is facing you and the worked stitches are held on the needle in your left hand. Proceed to make stitches as given above, with the initially empty needle held in your right hand.

PURL STITCH

1. With the yarn at the front, insert your right-hand needle from back to front into the 1st stitch on your left-hand needle.
2. Bring your working yarn over and around the point of your right-hand needle.
3. Draw a loop through and slide the 1st stitch off your left-hand needle while the new stitch is retained on your right-hand needle. Continue in this way to the end of the row.
4. To purl the next row, turn the work around so that the back is facing you and the worked stitches are held on the needle in your left hand. Proceed to make stitches as given above, with the initially empty needle held in your right hand.

INCREASING

YARN FORWARD

This method is used to make a stitch between two knit stitches. After the 1st knit stitch the yarn is at the back of the work. Bring the yarn forward between the needles. Knit the next stitch as usual.

YARN ROUND NEEDLE

1. This is used to make a stitch between 2 purl stitches. After the 1st purl stitch the yarn is at the front of the work. Take the yarn over then under the right-hand needle. Purl the next stitch as usual. 2. The same method is used to make a stitch between a knit and a purl stitch. After the knit stitch take the yarn under, over, then under the right-hand needle. Purl the next stitch as usual.

YARN BACK

This method is used to make a stitch between a purl and knit stitch. After the purl stitch the yarn is at the front of the work. Take yarn back over the right-hand needle. Knit the next stitch as usual.

MAKE 1

Pick up loop which lies before next stitch, place on left-hand needle and knit through back of loop.

DECREASING

KNIT 2 STITCHES TOGETHER (K2 TOG)

1. Insert the right-hand needle knitwise in to the 2nd and then the 1st stitch on the left-hand needle. Take the yarn under and over the point of the right-hand needle.
2. Draw the yearn through the 1st and 2nd stitches on the left-hand needle, discarding both stitches at the same time, thus ending with 1 stitch only.

PURL 2 STITCHES TOGETHER (P2 TOG)

1. Insert the right-hand needle purlwise into the 1st and then the 2nd stitch on the left-hand needle. Take the yarn over and under the point of the right-hand needle.
2. Draw the yarn through the 1st and 2nd stitches on the left-hand needle, discarding both stitches at the same time, thus ending with 1 stitch only.

SLIP 1, KNIT 1, PASS SLIPPED STITCH OVER (SL1, K1, PSSO)

1. Insert the right-hand needle into the next stitch on the left-hand needle as if to knit it. Slip the stitch off the needle onto the right-hand needle.
2. Knit the next stitch on the left-hand

needle as usual. With the point of the left-hand needle, lift up the slipped stitch and pass it over the stitch just knitted and off the needle.

JOINING IN A NEW YARN

It is generally best not to join yarns by knotting except where the join falls at the end of a row. For all mid row joins a much smoother finish can be obtained by using the double strand method: work the last stitch to be worked in the old yarn and then allow it to fall to the back of the work. Insert the right-hand needle into the next stitch on the left-hand needle leaving a short tail. Knit the stitch in the usual way and then work 2 or 3 more stitches using the new yarn doubled. (On the next row treat these as single stitches.) On the wrong side trim the end of the new yarn and darn in the end of the old yarn for a neat finish.

CASTING OFF

When you end a piece of knitting, such as a sleeve, or part of a piece of knitting, such as up to the neck, you must secure all the stitches by 'casting off'. This is preferably done on a knit row but you can employ the same technique on a purl or a rib row.

IN KNIT STITCH

1. Knit the first 2 stitches and insert the top of your left-hand needle through the 1st stitch.
2. Lift the 1st stitch over the 2nd stitch and discard it. Knit the next stitch and continue to lift the 1st stitch over the 2nd stitch to the end of the row. For the last stitch, cut your yarn, slip the end through the stitch and pull the yarn to fasten.

IN PURL STITCH

Purl the first 2 (and all subsequent) stitches and continue as for knit stitch above.

IN RIB STITCH

Knit or purl the first 2 (and all subsequent) stitches as they appear and continue as for knit stitch above.

PART KNITTING OR INTARSIA KNITTING (CHANGING COLOURS)

WORKING A KNIT ROW

Keep the yarns at the back of the work throughout and repeat the following for each new colour. Knit across the stitches in the 1st colour. Take this end of yarn over the top of the next colour to be used and drop it. Pick up the next colour under this strand of yarn and take it over the strand ready to knit the next stitch.

WORKING A PURL ROW

Keep the yarns at the front of the work throughout and repeat the following for each new colour. Purl across the stitches in the 1st colour. Take this end of yarn over the top of the next colour to be used and drop it. Pick up the next colour under this strand of yarn and take it over the strand ready to purl the next stitch. When working with small sections of colour in the centre of a graph, try using bobbins. Wind a quantity of yarn around the bobbin and place the end of the yarn through the slot to hold it. Unwind only enough yarn to knit the required stitches, then place the yarn in the slot, keeping the bobbin close to the work.

READING THE GRAPHS

Except where otherwise indicated, when working from graphs, read odd-numbered rows (knit rows) from right to left and even-numbered rows (purl rows) from left to right — 1 square equals one stitch.
Colour changes are indicated with a code to denote the colours. When working with a number of colours, you may find it easier to colour in the chart with the shades you intend to use before beginning to knit. It may also be helpful to first enlarge the graphs on a photocopier.

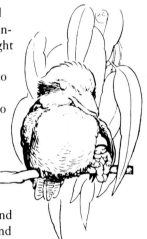

PICKING UP STITCHES

1. Stitches often need to be picked up round neck edges and armholes so that a neckband and armhole band can be knitted. To ensure they are picked up evenly, divide the edge into equal sections and mark them with pins.
2. Divide the number of sections into the number of stitches specified in the pattern and start picking up an equal number of stitches per section. Insert the top of the needle into a row end on vertical edges or a stitch on horizontal edges.
3. With the yarn at the back of the work, take it under and over the point of the needle, and draw a loop through.
4. Insert the tip of the needle into the next stitch or row end. Take the yarn under and over the point of the needle and draw a loop through.
Carry on in this way until the correct number of stitches have been picked up.

Oh!

Oo

Peeking

Pp

Sweet Pea

*Child's jumper with moss stitch and cable detail and Sweet Pea
Flower Baby motif embroidered in Knitting Stitch*

Measurements

To fit chest	cm	71	76
	in	28	30
Actual measurement	cm	85	93
Length to back neck	cm	50	56
Sleeve seam	cm	36	41

Materials

CLECKHEATON COUNTRY 8 PLY 50G BALLS

		11	12

1 pr each 4 mm (No 8), 3.25 mm (No 10) and
1 set of 3.25 mm (No 10) knitting needles or
the required size to give correct tension.
Cable needle. 2 stitch holders. DMC
tapestry wool and crewel wool in 12 shades
(see graph). Tapestry needle for embroidery.
4 mm (No 8) crochet hook.

Back

Using 3.25 mm needles, cast on 93 (101) sts.
1ST ROW K2, * P1, K1, rep from * to last st,
K1.
2ND ROW K1, * P1, K1, rep from * to end. **
Rep 1st and 2nd rows until work measures
5 (6) cm from beg, ending with a 2nd row
and inc 10 (12) sts evenly across last row.
103 (113) sts.
Change to 4 mm needles and beg moss
stitch patt.

1ST ROW K1, * P1, K1, rep from * to end.
2ND ROW P1, * K1, P1, rep from * to end.
3RD ROW As 2nd row.
4TH ROW As 1st row.
Rows 1 to 4 inclusive form moss stitch patt.
Cont in moss stitch patt until work
measures 48 (54) cm from beg, working
last row on wrong side.

Shape shoulders

Keeping patt correct, cast off 10 (11) sts at
beg of next 2 rows, 8 (9) sts at beg of foll 4
rows and 9 sts at beg of foll 2 rows.
Leave rem 33 (37) sts on a stitch holder.

Front

Work as for Back to **.
Rep 1st and 2nd rows until work measures
5 (6) cm from beg, ending with a 1st row.
NEXT ROW Rib 1 (5), inc in next st, * rib 4,
inc in next st, rep from * to last 1 (5) st/s,
rib 1 (5). 112 (120) sts.
Change to 4 mm needles.

Divide for side panel

1ST ROW K1, (P1, K1) 7 (9) times, turn.
Cont in moss stitch patt (as for Back) on
these 15 (19) sts for first side panel until
work measures 48 (54) cm from beg,
working last row on wrong side.

TENSION
*Before commencing your
garment it is essential to
first check your tension.
This garment has been
designed at a tension of
22 sts to 10 cm over st
st, using 4 mm needles,
and 24 sts to 10 cm over
moss stitch, using 4 mm
needles.*

ABBREVIATIONS
*C4F = Slip next 4 sts
onto a cable needle and
leave at front of work,
K4, then K4 from cable
needle.*

KEY *(one square equals one stitch)*

KNITTING STITCH
(tapestry wool)

◣ = 7640 *(1 skein)*

☒ = 7759 *(1 skein)*

⊡ = 7105 *(4 skeins)*

⊘ = 7853 *(5 skeins)*

⊡ = 7170 *(1 skein)*

☑ = 7491 *(1 skein)*

⊟ = 7241 *(1 skein)*

■ = Blanc *(1 skein)*

STEM STITCH
DMC crewel wool
8841 *(1 skein)*
7759 *(outlines)*

SATIN STITCH
7573 *(1 skein)*

➴ = Cornelli
pattern *(placement of
chain lengths)* 7548
(1 skein)

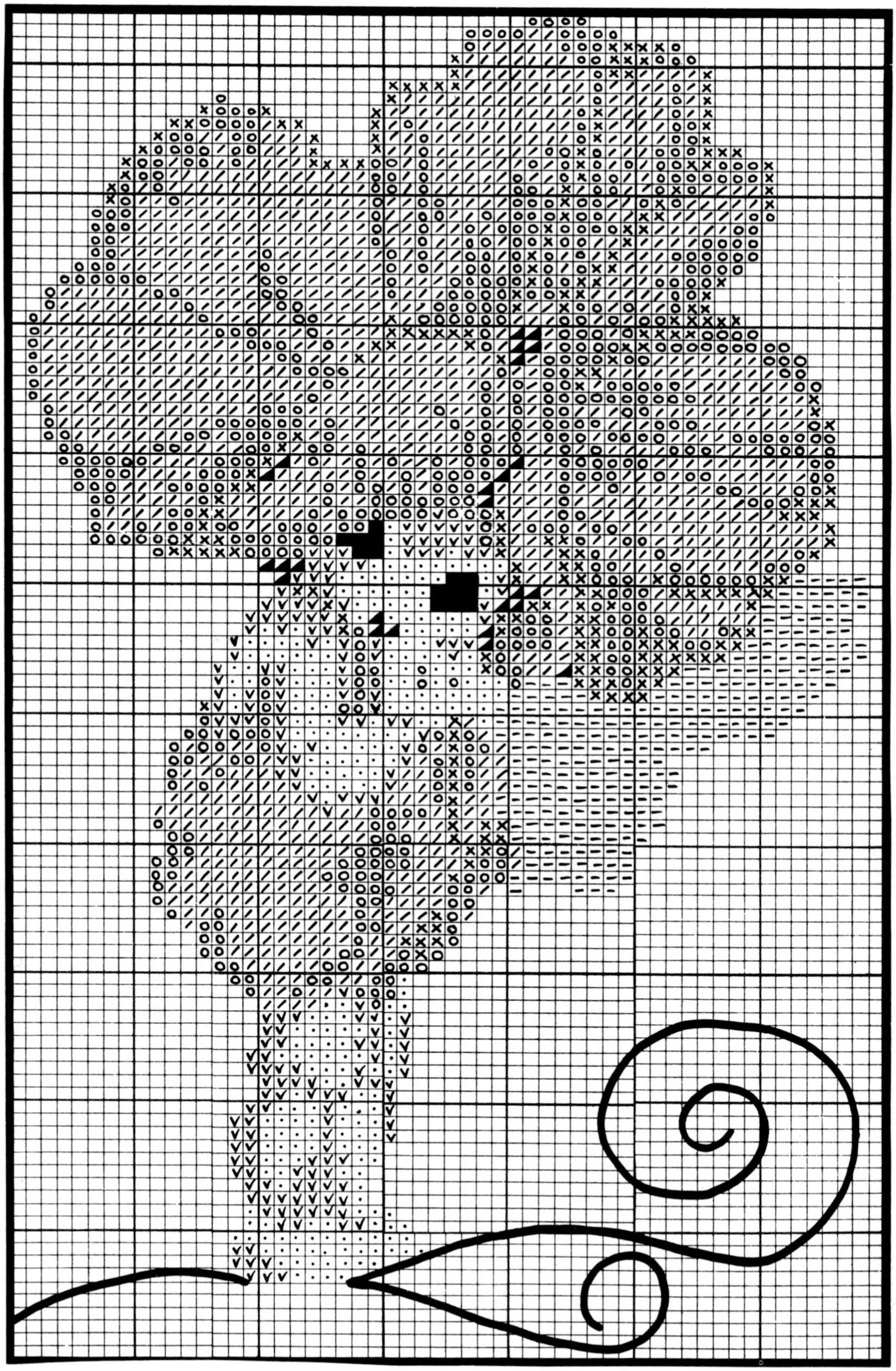

Shape shoulder
Keeping patt correct, cast off 10 (11) sts at beg of next row.
Work 1 row. Cast off rem 5 (8) sts.
With right side facing, join yarn to rem sts and cont as folls:
1st row P3, K8, P2, K56, P2, K8, P3, turn.
Cont on these 82 sts for centre panel.
2nd row K3, P8, K2, P56, K2, P8, K3.
3rd row P3, K8, P2, K56, P2, K8, P3.
Rep 2nd and 3rd rows once, then 2nd row once.
7th row P3, C4F, P2, K56, P2, C4F, P3.
Rep 2nd and 3rd rows 3 times, then 2nd row once.
Last 14 rows form patt for centre panel.
Cont in patt until work measures 43 (48.5) cm from beg, working last row on wrong side.

Shape neck
Next row Patt 32, turn.
Keeping patt correct, dec one st at neck edge in alt rows until 26 (25) sts rem.
Work 3 rows.

Shape shoulder
Cast off 7 (5) sts at beg of next row and 10 (11) sts at beg of foll alt row.
Work 1 row. Cast off rem 9 sts.
Slip next 18 sts onto a stitch holder and leave. Join yarn to rem sts and patt to end.
Keeping patt correct, dec one st at neck edge in alt rows until 26 (25) sts rem.
Work 4 rows.

Shape shoulder
Complete as for other shoulder.
With right side facing, join yarn to rem 15 (19) sts for second side panel and cont in moss stitch patt (as for Back) until work measures 48 (54) cm from beg, working last row on right side.

Shape shoulder
Complete as for first side panel.

Sleeves
Using 3.25 mm needles, cast on 37 (39) sts.
Work for 5 (6) cm in rib as for Back, ending with a first row.
Next row Rib 1 (2), inc in next st, * rib 1, inc in next st, rep from * to last 1 (2) st/s,

rib 1 (2). 55 (57) sts.
Change to 4 mm needles and beg moss stitch patt.
Cont in moss stitch patt (as for Back), inc one st at each end of 5th and foll 6th (4th) rows until there are 75 (67) sts, then in foll 8th (6th) rows until there are 81 (91) sts, working extra sts into patt.
Cont in patt without further shaping until side edge measures 36 (41) cm from beg, working last row on wrong side.

Shape top
Keeping patt correct, cast off 8 (9) sts at beg of next 8 rows.
Cast off rem 17 (19) sts.

Neckband
Using back stitch, join side panels to centre panel, then join shoulder seams (taking care to gather fabric slightly across top of cables and to match shaping).
With right side facing, using set of 3.25 mm needles, beg at left shoulder seam and knit up 87 (95) sts evenly around neck edge, including sts from stitch holders.
1st round * K1, P1, rep from * to end.
Rep 1st round until neckband measures 6 cm from beg.
Cast off loosely in rib.

To make up
Using Knitting Stitch and DMC tapestry wool, embroider motif from graph in st st section of front, noting that last row of graph should be 6 rows below beg of neck shaping. Using Stem Stitch and Satin Stitch, embroider facial features and outlines of motif as pictured. Using 4 mm crochet hook and grey-green shade of tapestry wool, make lengths of crocheted chain for Cornelli patt at lower edge of graph. Attach chain lengths as indicated on graph. Tie coloured threads 18 (20) cm down from centre of shoulder shaping at side edges of back and front to mark armholes. Using back stitch, sew in sleeves evenly between coloured threads, placing centres of sleeves to shoulder seams. Join side and sleeve seams. Fold neckband in half onto wrong side and slip stitch in position.

Gum Nut Baby

Child's jumper or cardigan with matching hat and adult's jumper with Gum Nut Baby motif embroidered in Knitting Stitch over stocking stitch

Measurements

To fit chest	cm	56	61
	in	22	24
Actual measurement	cm	66	73
Length to back neck (*Jumper*)	cm	37	41
Length to back neck (*Cardigan*)	cm	39	43
Sleeve seam	cm	22	26
Hat fits head	cm	54	54

Materials

CLECKHEATON COUNTRY 8 PLY 50G BALLS

Jumper	5	6
Cardigan	6	7
Hat	2	2

2 skeins each of DMC tapestry wool shades 7382 and 7384. 1 skein each of 6 shades (see graph). 1 skein of DMC crewel wool (see graph).
1 pr each 4 mm (No 8) and 3.25 mm (No 10) knitting needles or the required size to give correct tension. Tapestry needle for embroidery. 2 stitch holders and 1 set of 3.25 mm (No 10) knitting needles for Jumper. 1 stitch holder and 6 buttons for Cardigan.

CHILD'S JUMPER

Back

Using 3.25 mm needles, cast on 75 (83) sts.
1ST ROW K2, * P1, K1, rep from * to last st, K1.
2ND ROW K1, * P1, K1, rep from * to end.
Rep 1st and 2nd rows until work measures 4 (5) cm from beg, working last row on wrong side.
Change to 4 mm needles. **
Work in st st (1 row K, 1 row P) until work measures 36 (40) cm from beg, ending with a purl row.

Shape shoulders

Cast off 6 (7) sts at beg of next 6 rows, then 8 sts at beg of foll 2 rows.
Leave rem 23 (25) sts on a stitch holder.

Front

Work as for Back to **.
Work in st st until work measures 29 (32.5) cm from beg, ending with a purl row.

Shape neck

NEXT ROW K32 (36), turn.
*** Dec one st at neck edge in alt rows until 26 (29) sts rem.
Work 5 rows. ***

TENSION
Before commencing your garment it is essential to first check your tension. These garments have been designed at a tension of 22 sts to 10 cm over st st, using 4 mm needles.

Shape shoulder
Cast off 6 (7) sts at beg of next and foll alt rows 3 times in all.
Work 1 row. Cast off rem 8 sts.
With right side facing, slip next 11 sts onto stitch holder and leave. Join yarn to rem sts and knit to end.
Rep from *** to ***.
Work 1 row.

Shape shoulder
Complete as for other shoulder.

Sleeves

Using 3.25 mm needles, cast on 33 (35) sts.
Work 4 (5) cm in rib as for Back, ending with a 2nd row and inc 8 (10) sts evenly across last row. 41 (45) sts.
Change to 4 mm needles.
Work in st st, inc one st at each end of 5th and foll 4th rows until there are 55 (53) sts, then in foll 6th rows until there are 59 (63) sts.
Cont without further shaping until side edge measures 22 (26) cm from beg, ending with a purl row.

Shape top
Cast off 7 (8) sts at beg of next 6 rows.
Cast off rem sts.

Neckband

Using back stitch, join shoulder seams. With right side facing and using set of 3.25 mm needles, knit up 78 (84) sts evenly around neck edge, including sts from stitch holders.
1ST ROUND * K1, P1, rep from * to end.
Rep 1st round until neckband measures 5 cm from beg.
Cast off loosely in rib.

To make up

Using Knitting Stitch and DMC tapestry wool, embroider leaf motif from graph on top left side of front, noting that last row of graph is row before beg of shoulder shaping on garment. Using Stem Stitch and Back Stitch, embroider outlines of motif and Gum Nut Baby in colours as indicated. Using back stitch, sew in sleeves placing centre of sleeves to shoulder seams. Join side and sleeve seams. Fold neckband in half onto wrong side and slip stitch in position.

CHILD'S CARDIGAN

Back

Work as for Back of Jumper, working 2 cm more in length to beg of shoulder shaping.

Left Front

Using 3.25 mm needles, cast on 37 (41) sts.
Work for 4 (5) cm in rib as for Back of Jumper, ending with a 2nd row.
Change to 4 mm needles.
Work in st st until work measures 33 (36.5) cm from beg, ending with a knit row. ****

Shape neck
Cast off 6 sts at beg of next row.
Dec one st at neck edge in next row and foll alt rows until 26 (29) sts rem.
Work 1 row.

Shape shoulder
Complete as for Front of Jumper.

Right Front

Work as for Left Front to ****, ending with a purl row instead of a knit row.

Shape neck
Cast off 6 sts at beg of next row.
Dec one st at neck edge in alt row until 26 (28) sts rem.
Work 2 rows.

Shape shoulder
Complete as for Front of Jumper.

Sleeves

Work as for Sleeves of Jumper.

Right Front Band

Using 3.25 mm needles, cast on 11 sts.
Work 4 rows rib as for Back of Jumper.
5TH ROW Rib 4, K2 tog, yfwd, rib 5.
Work 17 (19) rows rib.
Rep last 18 (20) rows 3 times.
NEXT ROW As 5th row. *****
Work 14 (16) rows rib.
Leave sts on a spare needle. Do not break off yarn.

Left Front Band

Work as for Right Front Band to *****, omitting buttonholes.

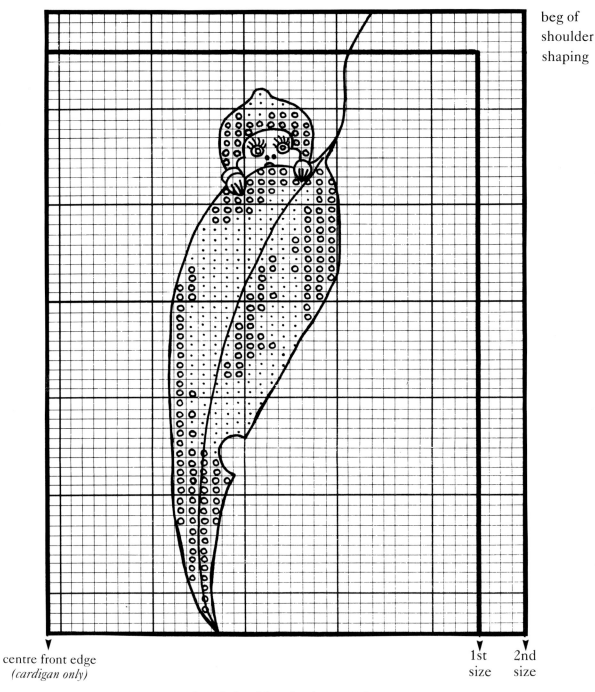

beg of
shoulder
shaping

centre front edge
(cardigan only)

1st
size

2nd
size

neck and shoulder shaping not shown

KEY *(one square equals one stitch)*

KNITTING STITCH *(tapestry wool)*

⊡ = 7382

⊙ = 7384

face and hands = 7191

SATIN STITCH *(tapestry wool)*

eyes = 7283 *(with white centre)*

eyelashes = 7421

mouth = 7759

STEM STITCH *(outlines)*

hat and outside of leaf = 7384
(tapestry wool)

centre of leaf = 7371 *(tapestry wool)*

DMC crewel wool 8841 for eyes,
nose and hands

Work 13 (15) rows rib. Break off yarn.
Leave sts on needle.

Neckband

Using back stitch, join shoulder seams.
With right side facing, using 3.25 mm
needles, holding right front band sts, knit
up 67 (73) sts evenly around neck edge
including sts from stitch holder, then rib
across left front band sts. 89 (95) sts.
Work 7 rows rib as for Back of Jumper, beg
with a 2nd row and work a buttonhole (as
before) in 4th row (6 buttonholes in all).
Cast off loosely in rib.

To make up

Using Knitting Stitch and DMC tapestry
wool, embroider leaf motif from graph on
left front, noting that last row of graph is
row before beg of shoulder shaping on
garment. Using Stem Stitch and Satin
Stitch, embroider outlines of motif and
Gum Nut Baby in colours as indicated.
Using back stitch, sew in sleeves placing
centre of sleeves to shoulder seams. Join
side and sleeve seams. Sew front bands in
position. Sew on buttons.

HAT

Using 3.25 mm needles, cast on 122 sts.
Work 20 rows st st.
Change to 4 mm needles.
Work 18 rows st st.

Shape crown

1ST ROW K1, * K2 tog, K18, rep from * to
last st, K1. 116 sts.
2ND AND ALT ROWS Purl.
3RD ROW K1, * K2 tog, K17, rep from * to
last st, K1. 110 sts.
5TH ROW K1, * K2 tog, K16, rep from * to
last st, K1. 104 sts.
7TH ROW K1, * K2 tog, K15, rep from * to
last st, K1. 98 sts.
Cont dec 6 sts in foll alt rows in this
manner until 20 sts rem.
Work 5 rows st st.
Break off yarn. Run end through rem sts
and draw up and fasten off securely.

To make up

Using back stitch, join back seam,
reversing seam along first 16 rows. Allow
first 16 rows to roll onto right side. Wind a
15 cm length of yarn around top of hat at
last dec row, secure end and thread back
into seam.

ADULT JUMPER

Measurements

To fit chest	cm	76:81	86:91	97:102
	in	30:32	34:36	38:40
Actual measurement	cm	103	113	124
Length to back neck	cm	66	67	68
Sleeve seam	cm	41	41	41

Materials

CLECKHEATON COUNTRY 8 PLY 50G BALLS

	14	15	16

1 pr each 4 mm (No 8), 3.25 mm (No 10) and 1 set of 3.25 mm (No 10) knitting needles or the required size to give correct tension. 3 skeins each of DMC tapestry wool shades 7382 and 7384. 1 skein each of 6 shades (see graph). 1 skein of DMC crewel wool (see graph). Tapestry needle for embroidery. 2 stitch holders.

Back

Using 3.25 mm needles, cast on 95 (107, 119) sts.
1st row K2, * P1, K1, rep from * to last st, K1.
2nd row K1, * P1, K1, rep from * to end.
Rep 1st and 2nd rows until work measures 8 cm from beg, ending with a 1st row.
Next row Rib 9 (6, 2), inc in next st, * rib 3 (4, 5), inc in next st, rep from * to last 9 (5, 2) sts, rib 9 (5, 2). 115 (127, 139) sts.
Change to 4 mm needles.
Cont in st st (1 row K, 1 row P) until work measures 64 (65, 66) cm from beg, working last row on wrong side.

Shape shoulders

Cast off 10 (12, 13) sts at beg of next 6 rows, then 11 (10, 12) sts at beg of foll 2 rows.
Leave rem 33 (35, 37) sts on a stitch holder.

Front

Work as given for Back until there are 22 (24, 24) rows less than back to beg of shoulder shaping.

Shape neck

Next row K50 (56, 62), turn.
*** Dec one st at neck edge in every row until 46 (50, 56) sts rem, then in foll alt rows until 41 (46, 51) sts rem.
Work 7 (9, 7) rows. ***

Shape shoulder

Cast off 10 (12, 13) sts at beg of next and foll alt row 3 times in all.
Work 1 row.
Cast off rem 11 (10, 12) sts.
Slip next 15 sts onto a stitch holder and leave. With right side facing, join yarn to rem sts and knit to end.
Rep from *** to ***.
Work 1 row.

TENSION
Before commencing your garment it is essential to first check your tension. This garment has been designed at a tension of 22 sts to 10 cm over st st, using 4 mm needles.

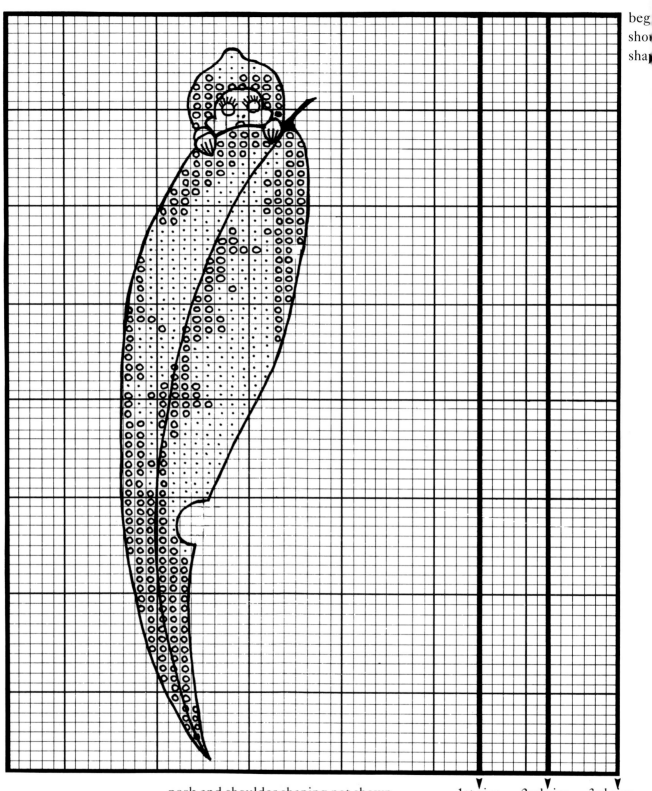

beg
sho
sha

neck and shoulder shaping not shown

1st size   2nd size   3rd size

side edge

KEY *(one square equals one stitch)*

KNITTING STITCH *(tapestry wool)*

⊡ = 7382

⊙ = 7384

face and hands = 7191

SATIN STITCH *(tapestry wool)*

eyes = 7283 *(with white centre)*

eyelashes = 7421

mouth = 7759

STEM STITCH *(outlines)*

hat and outside of leaf = 7384 *(tapestry wool)*

centre of leaf = 7371 *(tapestry wool)*

DMC crewel wool 8841 for eyes, nose

and hands

Shape shoulder
Complete as for other shoulder.

Sleeves

Using 3.25 mm needles, cast on 43 (45, 45) sts.
Work for 6 cm in rib as for Back, ending with a 1st row.
Next row Rib 6 (7, 7), inc in next st, * rib 1, inc in next st, rep from * to last 6 (7, 7) sts, rib 6 (7, 7). 59 (61, 61) sts.
Change to 4 mm needles.
Work in st st, inc one st at each end of 3rd and foll 4th (4th, alt) rows until there are 97 (105, 71) sts. 1st and 3rd sizes only – then in foll 6th (4th) rows until there are 101 (109) sts.
Cont without shaping until side edge measures 41 cm from beg, ending with a purl row.

Shape top
Cast off 10 sts at beg of next 8 rows.
Cast off rem 21 (25, 29) sts.

Neckband

Using back stitch, join shoulder seams.
With right side facing, using set of 3.25 mm needles, beg at left shoulder seam and knit up 90 (96, 98) sts evenly around neck edge, including sts from stitch holders.
1st round * K1, P1, rep from * to end.
Rep 1st round until neckband measures 5 cm from beg.
Cast off loosely in rib.

To make up

Using Knitting Stitch and DMC tapestry wool, embroider leaf motif from graph on top left side of front, noting that last row on graph is row before beg of shoulder shaping on garment. Using Stem Stitch and Satin Stitch, embroider outlines of motif and Gum Nut Baby in colours as indicated. Using back stitch, sew in sleeves, placing centre of sleeves to shoulder seams. Join side and sleeve seams. Fold neckband in half onto wrong side and slip stitch in position.

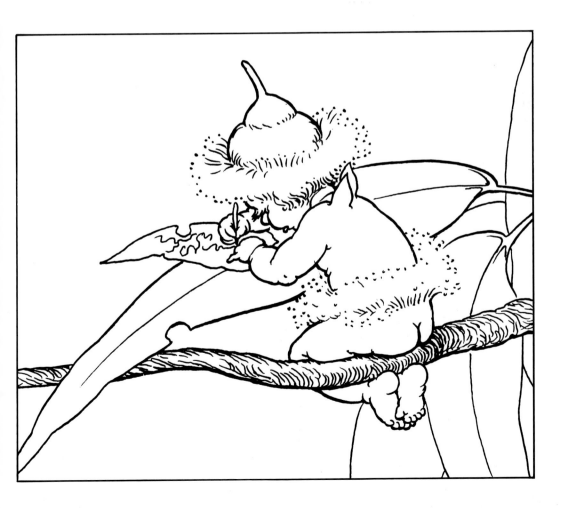

Snugglepot & Cuddlepie

Child's jumper with Snugglepot & Cuddlepie 'picture knit'
worked in stocking stitch from graph and
embroidered detail

Measurements

To fit chest	cm	66	71	76
	in	26	28	30
Actual measurement	cm	78	83	91
Length to back neck (*approx*)	cm	45	49	55
Sleeve seam	cm	31	36	41

Materials

CLECKHEATON 8 PLY PURE WOOL 50G BALLS

(*Navy*)	MC	4	5	6
(*Iris*)	C1	2	3	3
(*Red*)	C2	1	1	2
(*Cream*)	C3	1	1	1

DMC TAPESTRY WOOL

(*7171*)	C4	2	2	2
(*7548*)	C5	2	2	2
(*7769*)	C6	1	1	1
(*7283*)	C7	1	1	1
(*7759*)	C8	1	1	1
(*7421*)	C9	1	1	1

DMC CREWEL WOOL

(*8841*)	C10	1	1	1

1 pr each 4 mm (No 8), 3.25 mm (No 10) and 1 set of 3.25 mm (No 10) knitting needles or the required size to give correct tension. 2 stitch holders. Bobbins. Tapestry needle for embroidery.

Front

Using 3.25 mm needles and MC, cast on 79 (85, 95) sts.

1ST ROW K2, * P1, K1, rep from * to last st, K1.

2ND ROW K1, * P1, K1, rep from * to end.
Rep 1st and 2nd row until work measures 6 cm from beg, ending with a 2nd row and inc 8 sts evenly across last row. 87 (93, 103) sts.
Change to 4 mm needles.
** Using MC, work 4 rows st st (1 row K, 1 row P).

5TH ROW K3 (6, 3) MC, * K1 C3, K7 MC, rep from * to last 4 (7, 4) sts, K1 C3, K3 (6, 3) MC.
Using MC, work 5 rows st st, beg with a purl row.

11TH ROW K7 (2, 7) MC, * K1 C3, K7 MC, rep from * to last 0 (3, 0) sts, K0 (1, 0) C3, K0 (2, 0) MC.

12TH ROW Using MC, purl. **
Rep from ** to ** for 1st Patt.
Work 26 (38, 50) rows patt. ****
Work rows 1 to 52 inclusive from graph.
Using C1, work 4 (4, 10) rows st st.

Shape neck

NEXT ROW K37 (40, 45), turn.
*** Dec one st at neck edge in foll alt rows until 30 (33, 37) sts rem.
Work 9 (9, 7) rows. ***

TENSION

Before commencing your garment it is essential to first check your tension. This garment has been designed at a tension of 22 sts to 10 cm over st st, using 4 mm needles.

Shape shoulder
Cast off 10 (11, 12) sts at beg of next row and foll alt row.
Work 1 row. Cast off.
With right side facing, slip next 13 sts onto a stitch
holder and leave. Join yarn to rem sts and knit to end.
Rep from *** to ***.
Work 1 row.

Shape shoulder
Complete as for other shoulder shaping.

Back

Work as for Front to ****.
Using MC, work 1 row.
NEXT ROW Patt 56 (59, 64), using C2, purl to end.
NEXT ROW K40 (43, 48) C2, patt to end.
NEXT ROW Patt 37 (40, 45), using C2, purl to end.
NEXT ROW K57 (60, 65) C2, patt to end.
NEXT ROW Patt 24 (27, 32), using C2, purl to end.
Using C2, work 9 rows st st.
NEXT ROW P56 (59, 64) C2, using C1, purl to end.
NEXT ROW K40 (43, 48) C1, using C2, knit to end.
NEXT ROW P37 (40, 45) C2, using C1, purl to end.

NEXT ROW K57 (60, 65) C1, using C2, knit to end.
NEXT ROW P24 (27, 32) C2, using C1, purl to end.
Using C1, cont in st st until there are 8 rows less than
Front to beg of shoulder shaping.

Shape back neck
NEXT ROW K36 (39, 43), turn.
***** Dec one st at neck edge in every row until 30
(33, 37) sts rem.
Work 1 row. *****

Shape shoulder
Complete as for Front.
With right side facing, slip next 15 (15, 17) sts onto a
stitch holder and leave. Join yarn to rem sts and knit to
end.
Rep from ***** to *****.
Work 1 row.

Shape shoulder
Complete as for Front.

Sleeves
Using 3.25 mm needles and MC, cast on 37 (41, 47) sts.

NOTE *When changing colours in centre of row, twist the colour to be used underneath and to the right of colour just used, making sure both yarns are worked firmly at joins. Always change colours on wrong side of work so colour change does not show on right side. Use a separate ball of yarn for each section of colour. We suggest using bobbins. Wind a quantity of yarn around bobbin and place end through slot to hold. Unwind only enough yarn to knit required sts, then place yarn in slot, keeping bobbin close to work.*

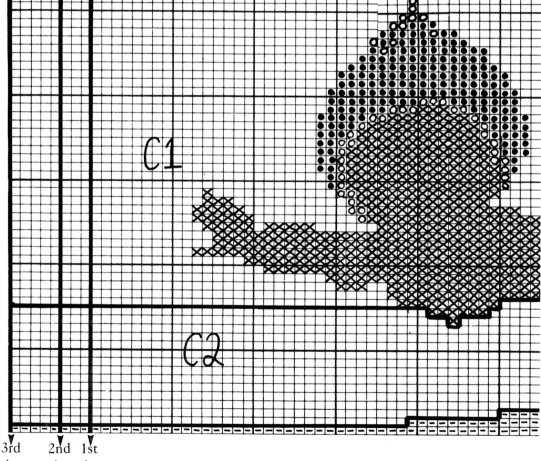

C1

C2

3rd
size

2nd
size

1st
size

Work 6 cm in rib as for Back, inc 10 (14, 16) sts evenly across last row. 47 (55, 63) sts. Change to 4 mm needles.
Cont in 1st patt as for 1st size of Front, inc one st at each end of 5th row and foll 6th (6th, 8th) rows until there are 65 (67, 79) sts, then in foll 8th (8th, 10th) row/s until there are 67 (77, 85) sts, working extra sts in 1st patt.
Cont in 1st patt without shaping until side edge measures 31 (36, 41) cm from beg, working last row on wrong side.

Shape top
Keeping patt correct, cast off 7 (9, 10) sts at beg of next 4 rows, then 8 (9, 11) sts at beg of foll 2 rows. Cast off rem sts.

Neckband
Using back stitch, join shoulder seams. With right side facing, using set of 3.25 mm needles and MC, beg at left shoulder seam, knit up 24 sts evenly along left side of front neck, knit across sts from front stitch holder, knit up 24 sts evenly along right side of front neck, knit up 10 sts evenly along right side of back neck, knit across sts from back neck stitch holder, then knit up 10 sts evenly along left side of back neck. 96 (96, 98) sts.
1ST ROUND * K1, P1, rep from * to end.
Rep 1st round until neckband measures 3 cm from beg.
Cast off loosely in rib.

To make up
Using C4, C5, and C6 and Knitting Stitch, embroider from graph. Using C7, C8 and C9 embroider facial features as pictured . Using C10 and Stem Stitch, embroider all outlines. Using back stitch, sew in sleeves placing centre of sleeve to shoulder seams. Join side and sleeve seams.

NOTE *When working in Fair Isle do not weave colours but carry colours not in use loosely across on wrong side of work. Always carry colours to end of row.*

KEY *(one square equals one stitch)*
⊟ = MC
v̄ = C3
⊠ = C4
● = C5
⊙ = C6
C1 and C2: work as indicated

51

41

31

21

11

1

C1

C1

C2

C2

1st size   2nd size   3rd size

Little Ragged Blossom

Child's jumper with Little Ragged Blossom 'picture knit' worked

in stocking stitch from graph and embroidered detail

Measurements

To fit chest	cm	71	76
	in	28	30
Actual measurement	cm	83	91
Length to back			
neck *(approx)*	cm	49	55
Sleeve seam	cm	38	41

Materials

CLECKHEATON COUNTRY 8 PLY 50G BALLS

(Cream)	MC	9	10

CLECKHEATON 8 PLY PURE WOOL 50G BALLS

(Dark Brown)	C1	1	1
(Rust)	C2	1	1
(Brown)	C3	1	1

DMC TAPESTRY WOOL

(7382)	C4	1	1
(7384)	C5	1	1
(7371)	C6	1	1
(7422)	C7	1	1
(7420)	C8	1	1
(7404)	C9	1	1
(7191)	C10	1	1
(7421)	C11	1	1
(7759)	C12	1	1
(7283)	C13	1	1

DMC CREWEL WOOL

(8841)	C14	1	1

1 pr each 4 mm (No 8), 3.25 mm (No 10) and 1 set of 3.25 mm (No 10) knitting needles or the required size to give correct tension. 2 stitch holders. Bobbins. Tapestry needle for embroidery.

Front

Using 3.25 mm needles and MC, cast on 81 (91) sts.
1ST ROW K2, * P1, K1, rep from * to last st, K1.
2ND ROW K1, * P1, K1, rep from * to end.
Rep 1st and 2nd rows until work measures 6 cm from beg, ending with a 2nd row and inc 12 sts evenly across last row. 93 (103) sts.
Change to 4 mm needles. ***
Work 12 (20) rows st st (1 row K, 1 row P).
Work rows 1 to 80 inclusive from graph.
Using MC, work 14 (24) rows st st.

Shape neck
NEXT ROW K40 (44), turn.
** Dec one st at neck edge in foll alt rows until 34 (38) sts rem.
Work 11 rows **.

Shape shoulder
Cast off 11 (13) sts at beg of next row and foll alt row.
Work 1 row. Cast off.
With right side facing, slip next 13 (15) sts

Tension
Before commencing your garment it is essential to first check your tension. This garment has been designed at a tension of 22 sts to 10 cm over st st, using 4 mm needles.

NOTE *When changing colours in centre of row, twist the colour to be used underneath and to the right of colour just used, making sure both yarns are worked firmly at joins. Always change colours on wrong side of work so colour change does not show on right side. Use a separate ball of yarn for each section of colour. We suggest using bobbins. Wind a quantity of yarn around bobbin and place end through slot to hold. Unwind only enough yarn to knit required sts, then place yarn in slot, keeping bobbin close to work.*

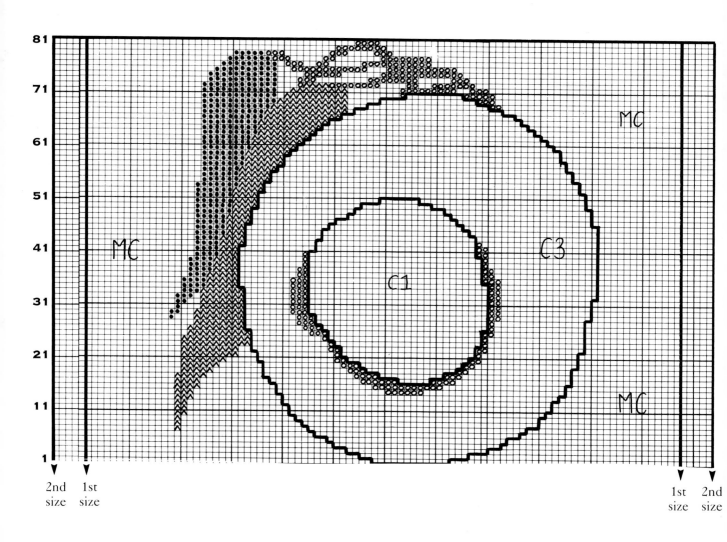

81
71
61
51
41
31
21
11
1

MC

MC

C3

C1

MC

2nd
size

1st
size

1st
size

2nd
size

KEY

KNITTING STITCH

O = C2

· = C4

∧ = C5

onto a stitch holder and leave. Join yarn to rem sts and knit to end.
Rep from ** to **.
Work 1 row.

Shape shoulder
Complete as for other shoulder shaping.

Back
Work as for Front to ***.
Using MC, cont in st st until work measures same as Front to beg of shoulder shaping, ending with a purl row.

Shape shoulders
Cast off 11 (13) sts at beg of next 4 rows, then 12 sts at beg of foll 2 rows.
Leave rem 25 (27) sts on a stitch holder.

Sleeves
Using 3.25 mm needles and MC, cast on 37 (39) sts.
Work for 6 cm in rib as for Back, ending with a 2nd row and inc 14 sts evenly across last row. 51 (53) sts.
Change to 4 mm needles.
Cont in st st, inc one st at each end of 3rd and foll 6th rows until there are 71 sts, then in foll 8th rows until there are 77 (81) sts.
Cont without shaping until side edge measures 38 (41) cm from beg, ending with a purl row.

Shape top
Cast off 9 (10) sts at beg of next 4 rows, then 9 sts at beg of foll 2 rows.
Cast off rem sts.

Neckband
Using back stitch, join shoulder seams. With right side facing, using set of 3.25 mm needles and MC, beg at left shoulder seam, knit up 86 (90) sts evenly around neck edge (including sts from stitch holders).
1ST ROUND * K1, P1, rep from * to end.
Rep 1st round until neckband measures 6 cm from beg.
Cast off loosely in rib.

To make up
Working from graph, embroider in Knitting Stitch using C2, C4 and C5. Using C6 and Stem Stitch, embroider veins on leaves. Using C10 and Knitting Stitch, embroider Little Ragged Blossom inside gum nut as illustrated. Using C11, C12 and C13, embroider facial features. Using C14 and Stem Stitch, embroider outlines of Ragged Blossom. Using C9 and Knitting Stitch, embroider hat. Using C7 and C8, work Turkey Rug Stitch for dress and around hat. Using C2 and Stem Stitch, embroider grain marks on gumnut.
Using back stitch, sew in sleeves placing centre of sleeves to shoulder seams. Join side and sleeve seams. Fold neckband in half onto wrong side and loosely slip stitch in position.

Mrs Bear & Wattle Baby

Child's jumper with Mrs Bear & Wattle Baby
'picture knit' worked in stocking stitch from graph
and embroidered detail

Measurements

To fit chest	cm	61	66
	in	24	26
Actual measurement	cm	73	78
Length to back			
neck *(approx)*	cm	41	44
Sleeve seam	cm	26	31

Materials

CLECKHEATON 8 PLY PURE WOOL 50G BALLS

(Blue)	MC	5	6
(Cream)	C1	1	1
(Rust)	C2	1	1
(Taupe)	C3	1	1
(Bone)	C4	1	1
(Charcoal)	C5	1	1
(Dark Brown)	C10	1	1

2 skeins each of C6 and C7 DMC tapestry wool and 1 skein each of 9 contrasting colours (see graph). 1 skein each of C13 and C14 DMC crewel wool.
1 pr each 4 mm (No 8), 3.25 mm (No 10) and 1 set of 3.25 mm (No 10) knitting needles or the required size to give correct tension. 2 stitch holders. Bobbins. Tapestry needle for embroidery.

Front

Using 3.25 mm needles and MC, cast on 69 (75) sts.
1ST ROW K2, * P1, K1, rep from * to last st, K1.
2ND ROW K1, * P1, K1, rep from * to end.
Rep 1st and 2nd rows until work measures 4 (5) cm from beg, ending with a 2nd row and inc 13 sts evenly across last row. 82 (88) sts.
Change to 4 mm needles. **
Work 2 (4) rows st st (1 row K, 1 row P).
Work rows 1 to 82 inclusive from graph.
Using MC, work 4 (6) rows st st.

Shape neck

NEXT ROW K34 (37), turn.
Dec one st at neck edge in foll alt rows until 29 (31) sts rem.
Work 11 rows.

Shape shoulder

Cast off 10 sts at beg of next row and foll alt row.
Work 1 row. Cast off.
With right side facing, slip next 14 sts onto a stitch holder and leave. Join yarn to rem sts and knit to end.
Complete to correspond with other side of neck, reversing all shapings.

TENSION
Before commencing your garment it is essential to first check your tension. This garment has been designed at a tension of 22 sts to 10 cm over st st, using 4 mm needles.

NOTE *When changing colours in centre of row, twist the colour to be used underneath and to the right of colour just used, making sure both yarns are worked firmly at joins. Always change colours on wrong side of work so colour change does not show on right side. Use a separate ball of yarn for each section of colour. We suggest using bobbins. Wind a quantity of yarn around bobbin and place end through slot to hold. Unwind only enough yarn to knit required sts, then place yarn in slot, keeping bobbin close to work.*

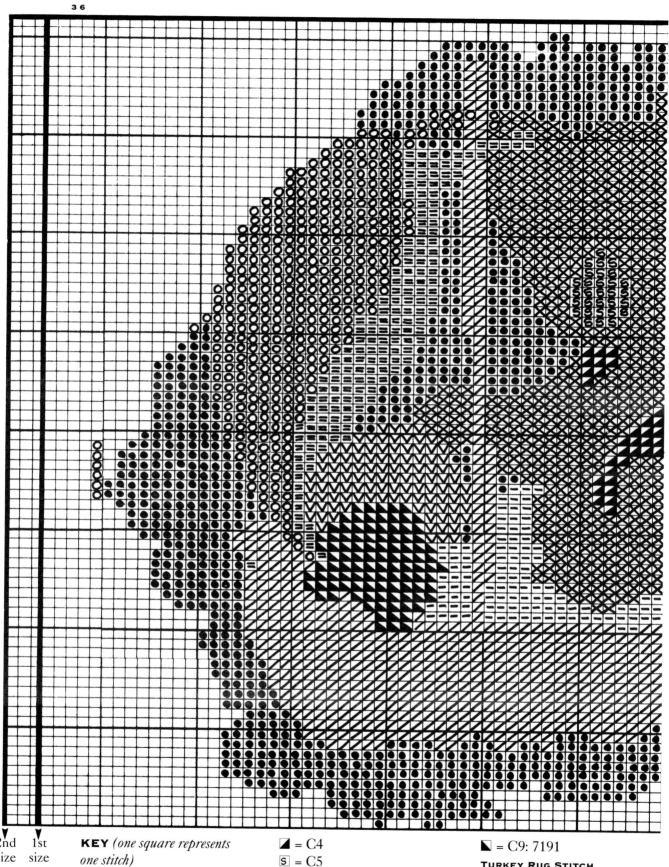

2nd size   1st size

KEY (one square represents one stitch)

☐ = MC
⚫ = C1
⧄ = C2
⊠ = C3

◢ = C4
Ⓢ = C5
⊟ = C10

KNITTING STITCH
Ⓞ = C6: 7768
⊜ = C7: 7700

◣ = C9: 7191

TURKEY RUG STITCH
Ⓥ = C8: 7784, 7971, 7973

STEM STITCH
outline of leaves = C11: 7890
outline of koala = C12: 7622

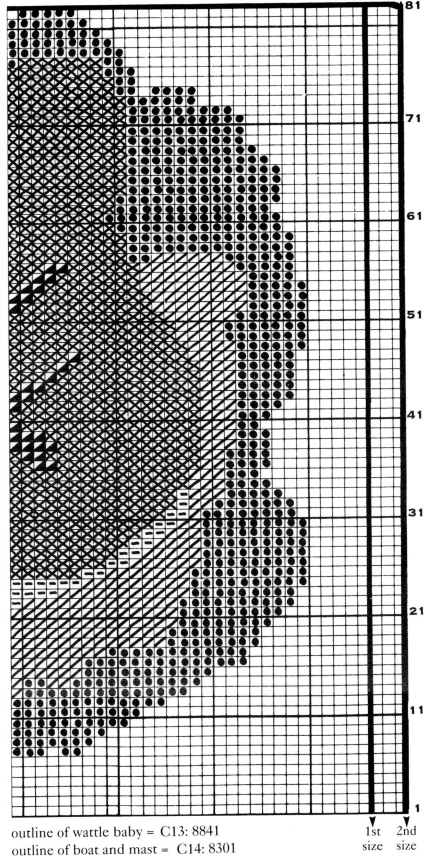

outline of wattle baby = C13: 8841
outline of boat and mast = C14: 8301

1st size   2nd size

Back

Work as for Front to **.
Cont in st st until work measures same as Front to beg of shoulder shaping, ending with a purl row.

Shape shoulders

Cast off 10 sts at beg of next 4 rows, then 9 (11) sts at beg of foll 2 rows.
Leave rem 24 (26) sts on a stitch holder.

Sleeves

Using 3.25 mm needles and MC, cast on 35 (37) sts.
Work for 4 cm in rib as for Front, ending with a 2nd row and inc 11 sts evenly across last row. 46 (48) sts.
Change to 4 mm needles.
Cont in st st, inc one st at each end of 5th row and foll 6th row/s until there are 50 (60) sts, then in foll 8th rows until there are 60 (68) sts.
Cont without shaping until side edge measures 26 (31) cm from beg, ending with a purl row.

Shape top

Cast off 7 (8) sts at beg of next 6 rows.
Cast off rem sts.

Neckband

Using back stitch, join shoulder seams.
With right side facing, using set of 3.25 mm needles and MC, beg at left shoulder seam, knit up 82 (88) sts evenly around neck edge (including sts from stitch holders).
1ST ROUND * K1, P1, rep from * to end.
Rep 1st round until neckband measures 5 cm from beg.
Cast off loosely in rib.

To make up

Using DMC tapestry wool embroider areas in Knitting Stitch as indicated on graph.
Embroider all other areas following stitch and colour guide as indicated on graph.
Using back stitch, sew in sleeves placing centre of sleeves to shoulder seams. Join side and sleeve seams. Fold neckband in half onto wrong side and loosely slip stitch in position.

SATIN STITCH
eyes of koala = C15: 7479

eyes of wattle baby = C16: 7314
lips of wattle baby = C17: 7108

Peek-a-boo

Child's cardigan in textured pattern with embroidered
Gum Nut Baby and Gum Leaf motif

Measurements

To fit chest	cm	61	66	71
	in	24	26	28
Actual measurement	cm	71	77	83
Length to back				
neck *(approx)*	cm	41	44	48
Sleeve seam	cm	26	31	36

Materials

CLECKHEATON 5 PLY MACHINE WASH 50G
BALLS

6	7	8

1 skein each of 8 contrasting colours in DMC
tapestry wool (see graph). 1 skein of DMC
crewel wool (see graph).
1 pr each 3.75 mm (No 9) and 3 mm (No 11)
knitting needles or the required size to give
correct tension. Stitch holder. Tapestry
needle for embroidery. 6 buttons.

Left Front

Using 3 mm needles, cast on 41 (45, 49)
sts.
1ST ROW K2, * P1, K1, rep from * to last st,
K1.
2ND ROW K1, * P1, K1, rep from * to end.
Rep 1st and 2nd rows until work measures
5 (5, 6) cm from beg, ending with a 2nd
row and inc 13 (13, 15) sts evenly across
last row. 54 (58, 64) sts.

Change to 3.75 mm needles.
1ST ROW Purl.
2ND ROW K1 (1, 0), * (K1, P1, K1) in next
st, P3 tog, rep from * to last 1 (1, 0) st/s, K1
(1, 0).
3RD ROW Purl.
4TH ROW K1 (1, 0), * P3 tog, (K1, P1, K1) in
next st, rep from * to last 1 (1, 0) st/s, K1
(1, 0).
Rows 1 to 4 inclusive form patt.
Cont in patt until work measures 24 (26,
29) cm from beg, working last row on right
side.
Keeping patt correct, cast off 6 sts at beg of
next and foll alt rows 8 (5, 6) times in all,
2nd and 3rd sizes only – then 7 sts at beg
of foll alt rows 3 times. 6 (7, 7) sts.
Cast off.

Right Front

Work as for Left Front noting to work last
row of patt on wrong side before working
shapings, and to work 1 more row before
casting off.

Left Front Yoke

Using 3.75 mm needles, cast on 5 sts.
Cont in st st (1 row K, 1 row P) casting on 5
sts at beg of 3rd and foll alt rows 8 (9, 7)
times in all. 3rd size only – then 6 sts at
beg of foll alt rows twice. 45 (50, 52) sts.

Work 4 rows st st, beg with a purl row.

Shape neck
Cast off 5 (6, 6) sts at beg of next row.
Dec one st at neck edge in next and foll alt rows until 35 (38, 40) sts rem.
Work 7 rows.

Shape shoulder
Cast off 12 (13, 13) sts at beg of next row and foll alt row.
Work 1 row. Cast off.

Right Front Yoke

Using 3.75 mm needles, cast on 5 sts.
Cont in st st, casting on 5 sts at beg of foll alt rows 8 (9, 7) times. 3rd size only – then 6 sts at beg of foll alt rows twice.
45 (50, 52) sts.
Work 4 rows st st.

Shape neck
Cast off 5 (6, 6) sts at beg of next row.
Dec one st at neck edge in foll alt rows until 35 (38, 40) sts rem.
Work 8 rows.

Shape shoulder
Complete as for Left Front Yoke.

Back

Using a flat seam, stitch yokes to fronts.
Using 3 mm needles, cast on 83 (91, 97) sts.
Work 5 (5, 6) cm in rib as for Left Front, ending with a 1st row.
NEXT ROW Rib 13 (3, 0), inc in next st * rib 1 (2, 2), inc in next st, rep from * to last 13 (3, 0) sts, rib 13 (3, 0). 112 (120, 130) sts.
Change to 3.75 mm needles.
1ST ROW Purl.
2ND ROW K0 (0, 1), * (K1, P1, K1) in next st, P3, tog, rep from * to last 0 (0, 1) st/s, K0 (0, 1).
3RD ROW Purl.
4TH ROW K0 (0, 1), * P3 tog, (K1, P1, K1) in next st, rep from * to last 0 (0, 1) st/s, K0 (0, 1).
Rows 1 to 4 inclusive form patt.
Cont in patt until work measures same as fronts to shoulder, working last row on wrong side.

Shape shoulders

Keeping patt correct, cast off 14 (15, 16) sts at beg of next 4 rows, then 13 (14, 16) sts at beg of foll 2 rows.
Leave rem 30 (32, 34) sts on a stitch holder.

Sleeves

Using 3 mm needles, cast on 45 (47, 49) sts.
Work 5 (5, 6) cm in rib as for Back, ending with a 2nd row and inc 15 (15, 17) sts evenly across last row. 60 (62, 66) sts.
Change to 3.75 mm needles.
1ST ROW Purl.
2ND ROW K0 (1, 1), * (K1, P1, K1) in next st, P3 tog, rep from * to last 0 (1, 1) st/s, K0 (1, 1).
3RD ROW Purl.
4TH ROW K0 (1, 1), * P3 tog, (K1, P1, K1) in next st, rep from * to last 0 (1, 1) st/s, K0 (1, 1).
Cont in patt as placed in last 4 rows, inc one st at each end of next and foll 4th rows until there are 70 (90, 100) sts, then in foll 6th rows until there are 82 (96, 106) sts, working extra sts in patt.
Cont in patt without shaping until side edge measures 26 (31, 36) cm from beg, working last row on wrong side.

Shape top

Keeping patt correct, cast off 10 (12, 13) sts at beg of next 6 rows.
Cast off rem sts.

Right Front Band

Using 3 mm needles and MC, cast on 11 sts.
1ST ROW K2, (P1, K1) 4 times, K1.
2ND ROW K1, (P1, K1) 5 times.
3RD ROW Rib 5, cast off 2 sts, rib 4.
4TH ROW Rib 4, cast on 2 sts, rib 5.
Work 22 (24, 26) rows rib.
Rep last 24 (26, 28) rows 3 times, then 3rd and 4th rows once. 5 buttonholes.
Work 18 (20, 22) rows rib.
Break off yarn. Leave sts on a spare needle.

Left Front Band

Work as for Right Front Band omitting buttonholes.
Break off yarn.

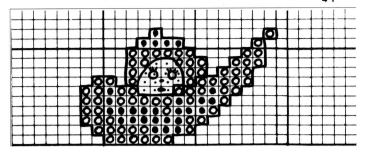

Neckband

Using back stitch, join shoulder seams. With right side facing, using 3 mm needles, rib across 11 sts from right front band, knit up 73 (79, 87) sts evenly along neck edge (including sts from back neck stitch holder), then rib across 11 sts from left front band. 95 (101, 109) sts.
Work 7 rows rib as given for lower band of Left Front, beg with a 2nd row and working a buttonhole (as before) in 4th and 5th rows.
Cast off loosely in rib.

To make up

Using back stitch, sew in sleeves placing centre of sleeves to shoulder seams. Join side and sleeve seams. Sew front bands in position. Sew on buttons. Using Knitting Stitch, embroider leaf, hat and flesh from graph, as illustrated. Work face and all outlines from graph, as illustrated.

KNITTING STITCH
☉ = 7384
● = 7382
· = 7191
SATIN STITCH
eyes = 7283
mouth = 7759
STEM STITCH
outside leaf = 7384
centre leaf = 7371
eyelashes = 7421
outline face = 8841

Bushland

Bush Fantasy

Child's stocking stitch gum nut and gum leaf design cardigan worked in complementary stripes and fair isle with embroidered bushland detail

Measurements

To fit chest	cm	61	66	71
	in	24	26	28
Actual measurement	cm	73	78	83
Length to back neck	cm	43	46	50
Sleeve seam	cm	26	31	36

Materials

CLECKHEATON COUNTRY 8 PLY 50G BALLS

(Purple)	MC	2	3	3
(Blue)	C1	3	4	4
(Green)	C2	2	2	3
(Cream)	C3	1	1	1

1 pr each 4.50 mm (No 7), 4 mm (No 8) and 3.25 mm (No 10) knitting needles or the required size to give correct tension. Stitch holder. 6 (7, 7) buttons. Tapestry needle for embroidery.

Back

Using 3.25 mm needles and C1, cast on 73 (77, 83) sts.

1ST ROW K2, * P1, K1, rep from * to last st, K1.

2ND ROW K1, * P1, K1, rep from * to end.

Rep 1st and 2nd rows until work measures 5 (5, 6) cm from beg, ending with a 2nd

row and inc 10 sts evenly across last row. 83 (87, 93) sts.

** Change to 4 mm needles.

Work 28 rows in st st (1 row K, 1 row P) in stripes of 12 rows C1, 8 rows MC, 2 rows C1, 2 rows C3, 2 rows C2 and 2 rows C1.

Change to 4.50 mm needles.

Work rows 1 to 13 inclusive from graph A.

Change to 4 mm needles and MC.

Cont in st st, beg with a purl row, until work measures 28 (30, 32) cm from beg, ending with a purl row.

Change to 4.50 mm needles.

Work rows 1 to 10 inclusive from graph D.

Change to 4 mm needles.

Using C2, work 4 rows st st. **

NEXT ROW K1 (3, 2) C2, * K1 C1, K3 C2, rep from * to last 2 (0, 3) sts, K1 (0, 1) C1, K1 (0, 2) C2.

Using C2, work 3 rows st st, beg with a purl row.

NEXT ROW K3 (1, 0) C2, * K1 C1, K3 C2, rep from * to last 0 (2, 1) st/s, K0 (1, 1) C1, K0 (1, 0) C2.

Using C2, work 3 rows st st, beg with a purl row.

Last 8 rows form remainder of patt.

Cont in patt until work measures 42 (45, 49) cm from beg, ending with a purl row.

TENSION

Before commencing your garment it is essential to first check your tension. This garment has been designed at a tension of 22 sts to 10 cm over st st, using 4 mm needles.

Shape neck
Keeping patt correct, cast off 6 (7, 7) sts at beg of next row.
Dec one st at neck edge in next and alt rows until 29 (30, 33) sts rem.
Work 1 (1, 3) row/s.

Shape shoulder
Cast off 7 (7, 8) sts at beg of next and alt rows 3 times in all.
Work 1 row.
Cast off.

Right Front
Work as given for Left Front to ***, noting to work graph C in place of graph B and that graph E has been reversed.
Next row * K3 C2, K1 C1, rep from * to last 1 (3, 2) st/s, K1 (3, 2) C2.
Using C2, work 3 rows st st, beg with a purl row.
Next row K1 C2, * K1 C1, K3 C2, rep from * to last 0 (2, 1) st/s, K0 (1, 1) C1, K0 (1, 0) C2.
Using C2, work 3 rows st st, beg with a purl row.
Last 8 rows form remainder of patt.
Cont in patt and complete to correspond with Left Front, working 1 row less before neck shaping and 1 row more before shoulder shaping.

Sleeves
Using 3.25 mm needles and C1, cast on 39 (41, 43) sts.
Work 5 (5, 6) cm in rib as for Back, ending with a 2nd row and inc 12 (16, 14) sts evenly across last row. 51 (57, 57) sts.
Change to 4 mm needles.
Cont in st st, in stripes of 10 (10, 14) rows C1, 8 rows MC, 2 rows C1, 2 rows C3, 2 rows C2, 12 (16, 20) rows C1 and 12 (14, 20) rows MC, at same time, inc one st at each end of 17th row and foll 6th (8th, 4th) row/s until there are 63 (63, 61) sts, 2nd and 3rd sizes only, then in foll (10th, 6th) rows until there are (67, 75) sts.
Work rows 1 to 10 inclusive from graph D as given for 1st size.
Cont in remainder of patt as given for 1st size of Back until side edge measures 26 (31, 36) cm from beg, working last row on wrong side.

Shape shoulders
Keeping patt correct, cast off 7 (7, 8) sts at beg of next 6 rows, then 8 (9, 9) sts at beg of foll 2 rows.
Leave rem 25 (27, 27) sts on a stitch holder.

Left Front
Using 3.25 mm needles and C1, cast on 37 (39, 41) sts.
Work 5 (5, 6) cm in rib as given for lower band of Back, ending with a 2nd row and inc 4 (4, 5) sts evenly across last row. 41 (43, 46) sts.
Work as given for Back from ** to **, working graph B in place of graph A and graph E in place of graph D. ***
Next row K1 (3, 2) C2, * K1 C1, K3 C2, rep from * to end.
Using C2, work 3 rows st st, beg with a purl row.
Next row K3 (1, 0) C2, * K1 C1, K3 C2, rep from * to last 2 sts, K1 C1, K1 C2.
Using C2, work 3 rows st st, beg with a purl row.
Last 8 rows form remainder of patt.
Cont in patt until there are 13 (13, 15) rows less than Back to beg of shoulder shaping.

Shape top

Keeping patt correct, cast off 7 (8, 9) sts at beg of next 6 rows.
Cast off rem sts.

Left Front Band (BOY), Right Front Band (GIRL)

Using back stitch, join shoulder seams.
Using 3.25 mm needles and C1, cast on 11 sts.

1ST ROW K2, (P1, K1) 4 times, K1.
2ND ROW K1, (P1, K1) 5 times.
3RD ROW Rib 5, cast off 2 sts, rib 4.
4TH ROW Rib 4, cast on 2 sts, rib 5.
Work 16 (18, 20) rows rib.
Rep last 18 (20, 22) rows 3 (4, 4) times more, then 3rd and 4th rows once. 5 (6, 6) buttonholes.
Work 12 (14, 16) rows rib.
Leave sts on a spare needle.

Right Front Band (BOY), Left Front Band (GIRL)

Work as for other band omitting buttonholes.

Neckband

Using back stitch, sew front bands in position. With right side facing, using 3.25 mm needles and C1, rib across right front band sts, knit up 63 (69, 75) sts evenly around neck edge (including sts from back neck stitch holder), then rib across left front band sts. 85 (91, 97) sts.
Work 9 rows rib as for lower band of Back, beg with a 2nd row and working a buttonhole (as before) in 4th and 5th rows.
Cast off loosely in rib.

To make up

Using back stitch, sew in sleeves placing centre of sleeves to shoulder seams. Join side and sleeve seams. Sew on buttons. Using C1 and Knitting Stitch, embroider gum nuts from graph F on back, fronts and sleeves as illustrated, placing gum nuts approx 3 sts from centre fronts.

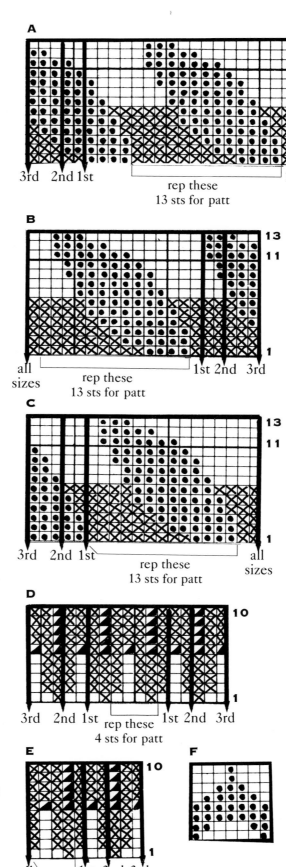

KEY *(one square equals one stitch)*

☐ = MC
☒ = C1
◪ = C2
⊡ = C3

NOTE
When working from graphs for Back, Left Front and Sleeves, work odd numbered rows (knit rows) from right to left and even numbered rows (purl rows) from left to right. When working from graphs C and E for Right Front, work odd numbered rows (knit rows) from left to right and even numbered rows (purl rows) from right to left.

Wattle Blossom

Child's cardigan worked in stocking stitch with

embroidered wattle blossom detail

Measurements

To fit chest	cm	61	66	71
	in	24	26	28
Actual measurement	cm	71	76	81
Length to back neck	cm	39	42	46
Sleeve seam	cm	6	6	7

Materials

CLECKHEATON COUNTRY 8 PLY 50G BALLS

	MC	5	6	7
DMC TAPESTRY WOOL				
(7392)	C1	1	1	1
(7784)	C2	1	1	1
(7971)	C3	1	1	1
(7973)	C4	1	1	1

1 pr each 4 mm (No 8) and 3.25 mm (No 10) knitting needles or the required size to give correct tension. Stitch holder. Tapestry needle for embroidery. 6 (6, 7) buttons.

Back

Using 3.25 mm needles and MC, cast on 69 (75, 81) sts.
1ST ROW K2, * P1, K1 rep from * to last st, K1.
2ND ROW K1, * P1, K1, rep from * to end.
Rep 1st and 2nd rows until work measures 7 (8, 8) cm from beg, ending with a 2nd row and inc 10 sts evenly across last row. 79 (85, 91) sts.

Change to 4 mm needles.
Work in st st (1 row K, 1 row P) until work measures 25 (27, 30) cm from beg, ending with a purl row.

Shape armholes

Cast off 5 sts at beg of next 2 rows.
Dec one st at each end of next and foll alt rows until 61 (65, 71) sts rem.
Work 33 (35, 37) rows.

Shape shoulders

Cast off 6 (6, 7) sts at beg of next 4 rows, then 6 (7, 8) sts at beg of foll 2 rows.
Leave rem 25 (27, 27) sts on a stitch holder.

Left Front

Using 3.25 mm needles and MC, cast on 35 (37, 41) sts.
Work for 7 (8, 8) cm in rib as for Back, ending with a 2nd row and inc 4 (5, 4) sts evenly across last row. 39 (42, 45) sts.
Change to 4 mm needles.
Cont in st st until work measures 25 (27, 30) cm from beg, ending with a purl row. **

Shape armhole

Cast off 5 sts at beg of next row.
Dec one st at armhole edge in alt rows until 30 (32, 35) sts rem.
Work 18 (18, 20) rows.

Shape neck
Cast off 6 sts at beg of next row.
Dec one st at neck edge in next and alt
rows until 18 (19, 22) sts rem.
Work 3 rows.

Shape shoulder
Cast off 6 (6, 7) sts at beg of next row and
foll alt row.
Work 1 row. Cast off.

Right Front

Work as given for Left Front to **.
Work 1 row.

Shape armhole
Cast off 5 sts at beg of next row.
Dec one st at armhole edge in next and alt
rows until 30 (32, 35) sts rem.
Work 17 (17, 19) rows.

Shape neck
Cast off 6 sts at beg of next row.
Dec one st at neck edge in alt rows until
18 (19, 22) sts rem.
Work 4 rows.

Shape shoulder
Complete as for Left Front.

Sleeves

Using 3.25 mm needles and MC, cast on
47 (49, 51) sts.
Work for 3 (3, 4) cm in rib as given for
Back, ending with a 2nd row and inc 12 sts
evenly across last row. 59 (61, 63) sts.
Change to 4 mm needles.
Cont in st st, until work measures 6 (6, 7)
cm from beg, ending with a purl row.

Shape top
Cast off 3 sts at beg of next 2 rows.
Dec one st at each end of next and foll 4th
rows until 43 (43, 45) sts rem, then in foll
alt rows until 23 sts rem.
Next row P1, (P2 tog) 11 times. 12 sts.
Cast off.

Left Front Band

Using 3.25 mm needles and MC, cast on
11 sts.
1st row K2, (P1, K1) 4 times, K1.
2nd row K1, (P1, K1) 5 times. ***
Rep 1st and 2nd rows 49 (54, 59) times.

100 (110, 120) rows in all. Break off yarn.
Leave sts on a spare needle.

Right Front Band
Work as given for Left Front Band to ***.
Rep 1st and 2nd rows once.
5TH ROW Rib 5, cast off 2 sts, rib 4.
6TH ROW Rib 4, cast on 2 sts, rib 5.
Work 18 (20, 18) rows rib.
Rep last 20 (22, 20) rows 3 (3, 4) times
more, then 5th and 6th rows once. 5 (5, 6)
buttonholes.
Work 15 (17, 15) rows rib.
Leave sts on needle. Do not break off
yarn.

Neckband
Using back stitch, join shoulder seams.
Sew front bands in position. With right
side facing, using 3.25 mm needles and
MC and holding right front band sts , knit
up 67 (71, 75) sts evenly around neck edge
(including sts from back neck stitch
holder), then rib across left front band sts.
89 (93, 97) sts.
Work 9 rows rib as given for lower band of
Back, beg with a 2nd row and working a
buttonhole (as before) in 4th and 5th rows.
Cast off loosely in rib.

To make up
Using C2, C3 and C4, embroider Bullion
Stitch for wattle on back, front and sleeves
at random. Using C1 and Satin Stitch,
embroider leaves to wattle as pictured.
Using back stitch, join side and sleeve
seams. Sew in sleeves gathering any extra
fullness across top of sleeves. Sew on
buttons.

Bushland Belle

Small child's jumper worked in stocking stitch with delicate picot edging and embroidered bushland blossom detail

Measurements

To fit chest	cm	56	61
	in	22	24
Actual measurement	cm	66	73
Length to shoulder	cm	37	41
Sleeve seam	cm	22	26

Materials

CLECKHEATON 5 PLY MACHINE WASH 50G BALLS

		MC	4	5
DMC TAPESTRY WOOL				
(7506)	C1	1	1
(7489)	C2	1	1
(7700)	C3	1	1
(7971)	C4	1	1
(7973)	C5	1	1
(7784)	C6	1	1
(7392)	C7	1	1
(7106)	C8	1	1
(7666)	C9	1	1
(7107)	C10	1	1
(7606)	C11	1	1
(7769)	C12	1	1

1 pr each 3.75 mm (No 9) and 3 mm (No 11) knitting needles or the required size to give correct tension. 2 stitch holders. Tapestry needles for embroidery. 3 buttons.

Back

Using 3 mm needles and MC, cast on 87 (97) sts.
Work 6 rows st st (1 row K, 1 row P).
NEXT ROW (Foldline) K1, * yfwd, K2 tog, rep from * to end.
Work 5 rows st st, beg with a purl row.
Change to 3.75 mm needles. ***
Cont in st st until work measures 35 (39) cm from foldline, ending with a purl row.

Shape back neck

NEXT ROW K36 (40), turn.
** Dec one st at neck edge in every row until 30 (34) sts rem.
Work 1 row. **

Shape shoulder

Cast off 10 (11) sts at beg of next row and foll alt row.
Work 1 row. Cast off.
With right side facing, slip next 15 (17) sts onto a stitch holder and leave. Join yarn to rem sts and knit to end.
Rep from ** to **.
Work 1 row.

Shape shoulder

Complete as for other shoulder shaping.

TENSION

Before commencing your garment it is essential to first check your tension. This garment has been designed at a tension of 26 sts to 10 cm over st st, using 3.75 mm needles.

Front

Work as for Back to ***.
Cont in st st until there are 18 (20) rows less than back to shoulder shaping.

Shape neck

NEXT ROW K36 (40), turn.
**** Dec one st at neck edge in every row 4 (2) times, then in foll alt rows 2 (4) times. 30 (34) sts.
Work 1 row. ****
NOTE This side of neck is 8 rows lower to accommodate shoulder opening.

Shape shoulder

Complete as for Back shoulder shaping.
With right side facing, slip next 15 (17) sts onto a stitch holder and leave. Join yarn to rem sts and knit to end.
Rep from **** to ****.
Work 9 rows.

Shape shoulder

Complete as for other shoulder.

Sleeves

Using 3 mm needles and MC, cast on 39 (41) sts.
Work 6 rows st st.
NEXT ROW (Foldline) K1, * yfwd, K2 tog, rep from * to end.
Work 5 rows st st, beg with a purl row.
Change to 3.75 mm needles.
Cont in st st, inc one st at each end of 3rd row and foll 4th rows until there are 63 (57) sts, then in foll 6th row/s until there are 65 (69) sts.
Cont without shaping until side edge measures 22 (26) cm from foldline, ending with a purl row.

Shape top

Cast off 8 sts at beg of next 6 rows.
Cast off rem sts.

Neckband

Using back stitch, join right shoulder seam.
With right side facing, using 3 mm needles and MC, knit up 14 (16) sts evenly along left side of Front neck, knit across sts from front stitch holder, knit up 22 (24) sts evenly along right side of Front neck, knit up 11 sts evenly along right side of Back neck, knit across sts from back neck stitch holder inc one st at end, then knit up 11 sts evenly along left side of Back neck. 87 (95) sts.
1ST ROW K1, * P1, K1, rep from * to end.
2ND ROW K2, * P1, K1, rep from * to last st, K1.
Rep 1st and 2nd rows twice, then 1st row once.
Cast off loosely in rib.

Front Shoulder Band

With right side facing, using 3 mm needles and MC, knit up 37 (41) sts evenly along shoulder and side edge of neckband.
Work 3 rows rib as for Neckband.
4TH ROW Rib 3 (4), [yfwd, K2 tog, rib 13 (14)] twice, yfwd, K2 tog, rib 2 (3).
3 buttonholes.
Work 3 rows rib.
Cast off loosely in rib.

Back Shoulder Band

Work as for Front Shoulder Band omitting buttonholes.

To make up

Using C1, C2 and C3 and Satin and Stem Stitch, embroider boronia on back, front and sleeves as pictured. Using C4, C5 and C6, embroider Bullion Stitch wattle. Using C7, embroider Satin Stitch leaves to wattle. Using C8, C9, C10 and C11, embroider gum blossom using Turkey Rug Stitch. Using C12, embroider Satin and Stem Stitch leaves to gum blossom as pictured. Place front shoulder band over back shoulder band and oversew at armhole edge. Using back stitch, sew in sleeves placing centre of sleeves to shoulder seams. Join side and sleeve seams. Sew on buttons.

Wattle Beauty

Adult's jumper with dolman sleeves and embroidered wattle detail

Measurements

To fit chest		76:81	86:91	97:102
	cm			
	in	30:32	34:36	38:40
Actual measurement	cm	101	111	121
Length to back neck *(approx)*	cm	66	68	68
Sleeve fits	cm	43	43	43

Materials

CLECKHEATON COUNTRY 8 PLY 50G BALLS

	MC	17	18	19
	C1	1	1	1

DMC TAPESTRY WOOLS

(7971)	C2	2	2	2
(7973)	C3	2	2	2
(7784)	C4	2	2	2

1 pr each 4 mm (No 8), 3.25 mm (No 10) and 1 set 3.25 mm (No 10) knitting needles or the required size to give correct tension. 2 stitch holders. Tapestry needle for embroidery.

Back

Using 3.25 mm needles and MC, cast on 97 (107, 115) sts.
1ST ROW K2, * P1, K1, rep from * to last st, K1.
2ND ROW K1, * P1, K1, rep from * to end.
Rep 1st and 2nd rows until work measures 8.5 cm from beg, ending with a 1st row.
NEXT ROW Rib 3 (2, 0), inc in next st, * rib 5, inc in next st, rep from * to last 3 (2, 0) sts, rib 3 (2, 0). 113 (125, 135) sts.
Change to 4 mm needles.
Work 16 rows st st (1 row K, 1 row P).
Cont in st st, inc one st at each end of next and foll 8th rows until there are 129 (141, 151) sts.
Inc one st at each end of alt rows until there are 139 (151, 161) sts.
Work 1 row.
Cast on 3 sts at beg of next 8 rows, then cast on 5 sts at beg of foll 8 rows, then cast on 10 sts at beg of foll 6 rows.
263 (275, 285) sts. **
Work 64 (70, 70) rows.

Shape top of sleeves and shoulders

Cast off 29 (30, 31) sts at beg of next 6 rows, then 28 (31, 31) sts at beg of foll 2 rows.
Leave rem 33 (33, 37) sts on a stitch holder.

TENSION

Before commencing your garment it is essential to first check your tension. This garment has been designed at a tension of 22 sts to 10 cm over st st, using 4 mm needles.

Front

Work as for Back to **.
Work 40 (44, 42) rows.

Shape neck

NEXT ROW K124 (130, 134), turn.
*** Dec one st at neck edge in alt rows 9
(9, 10) times.
115 (121, 124) sts.
Work 5 (7, 7) rows. ***

Shape top of sleeve and shoulder

Cast off 29 (30, 31) sts at beg of next row
and foll alt rows 3 times in all.
Work 1 row.
Cast off rem 28 (31, 31) sts.
Slip next 15 (15, 17) sts onto a stitch holder
and leave. With right side facing, join yarn
to rem sts and knit to end.
Rep from *** to ***.
Work 1 row.

1st round * K1, P1, rep from * to end.
Rep 1st round until neckband measures 6 cm from beg.
Cast off loosely in rib.

Wristband

With right side facing, using 3.25 mm needles and MC, knit up 95 (103, 103) sts evenly along straight (side) edge of sleeves.
1st row P3 (5, 5), * K2 tog, rep from * to last 2 (4, 4) sts, P2 (4, 4). 45 (47, 47) sts.
Work in rib as for Back, until wristband measures 8.5 cm from beg, ending with a 2nd row.
Cast off loosely in rib.

To make up

Using C2, C3 and C4 embroider clusters of wattle in Bullion Stitch on front as pictured. Using 4 mm hook and C1, make 12 crocheted chain lengths ranging in length from 12 – 22 cm (or as desired). Attach chains to front of garment. Using back stitch, join side and lower sleeve seams. Fold neckband in half onto wrong side and slip stitch loosely in position.

Shape top of sleeve and shoulder
Complete as for other side.

Neckband

Using back stitch, join top of sleeves and shoulder seams. With right side facing, using set of 3.25 mm needles and MC, beg at left shoulder seam and knit up 104 (108, 114) sts evenly around neck edge (including sts from stitch holders).

Spring Blossoms

Diamond cable patterned jumper for adult or child with embroidered boronia, gum blossom and wattle detail

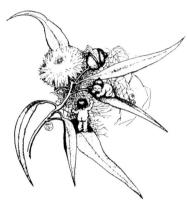

Measurements

To fit chest						
	cm	66	71	76:81	86:91	97:102
	in	26	28	30:32	34:36	38:40
Actual measurement	cm	78	83	106	116	127
Length to back neck	cm	44	48	65	66	67
Sleeve seam	cm	33	38	43	43	43

Materials

CLECKHEATON 8 PLY PURE WOOL 50G BALLS

MC		8	9	15	16	17

DMC TAPESTRY WOOL

(7392)	C1	1	1	1	1	1
(7784)	C2	1	1	1	1	1
(7971)	C3	1	1	1	1	1
(7973)	C4	1	1	1	1	1
(7506)	C5	1	1	1	1	1
(7707)	C6	1	1	1	1	1
(7489)	C7	1	1	1	1	1
(7107)	C8	1	1	1	1	1
(7606)	C9	1	1	1	1	1
(7666)	C10	1	1	1	1	1
(7106)	C11	1	1	1	1	1

1 pr each 4 mm (No 8), 3.25 mm (No 10) and 1 set 3.25 mm (No 10) knitting needles or the required size to give correct tension. 2 stitch holders. Tapestry needle for embroidery.

Back

Using 3.25 mm needles and MC, cast on 85 (85, 115, 125, 135) sts.

1ST ROW (K1 tbl, P1) twice, K1 tbl, * P5, (K1 tbl, P1) twice, K1 tbl, rep from * to end.

2ND ROW (P1 tbl, K1) twice, P1 tbl, * K5, (P1 tbl, K1) twice, P1 tbl, rep from * to end.

Rep 1st and 2nd rows until work measures 8 (8, 10, 10, 10) cm from beg, ending with a 2nd row and inc 10 (16, 14, 16, 20) sts evenly across last row.

95 (101, 129, 141, 155) sts.

Change to 4 mm needles.

1ST ROW K3 (6, 2, 8, 1), K2 tog, K2, yfwd, K1, yfwd, K2, (K2 tog tbl, K5) 0 (0, 0, 0, 1) time/s, * K4, K2 tog, K2, yfwd, K1, yfwd, K2, K2 tog tbl, K5, rep from * last 2 (5, 1, 7, 14) st/s, (K4, K2 tog, K2, yfwd, K1, yfwd, K2, K2 tog tbl) 0 (0, 0, 0, 1) time/s, K2 (5, 1, 7, 1).

2ND AND ALT ROWS Purl.

3RD ROW K3 (6, 2, 8, 0), (K2 tog, K2, yfwd, K3, yfwd, K2, K2 tog tbl, K4) 0 (0, 0, 0, 1) time/s, * K3, K2 tog, K2, yfwd, K3, yfwd, K2, K2 tog tbl, K4, rep from * to last 2 (5, 1, 7, 14) st/s, (K3, K2 tog, K2, yfwd, K3, yfwd, K2, K2 tog tbl) 0 (0, 0, 0, 1) time/s, K2 (5, 1, 7, 0).

5TH ROW K3 (6, 2, 1, 8), (yfwd, K2, K2 tog tbl, K3) 0 (0, 0, 1, 1) time/s, * K2, K2 tog, K2, yfwd, K5, yfwd, K2, K2 tog tbl, K3, rep

TENSION

Before commencing your garment it is essential to first check your tension. These garments have been designed at a tension of 22 sts to 10 cm over st st, using 4 mm needles.

ABBREVIATIONS

MI = Pick up loop which lies before next st, place on left hand needle and knit through back of loop.

from * to last 2 (5, 1, 7, 14) st/s, (K2, K2 tog, K2, yfwd) 0 (0, 0, 1, 1) time/s, K2 (5, 1, 1, 8).

7TH ROW K0 (0, 0, 1, 8), (yfwd, K3, K2 tog tbl) 0 (0, 0, 1, 1) time/s, K3 (6, 2, 2, 2), * K1, K2 tog, K3, yfwd, K5, yfwd, K3, K2 tog tbl, K2, rep from * to last 2 (5,1,7,14) st/s, (K1, K2 tog, K3, yfwd) 0 (0, 0, 1, 1) time/s, K2 (5, 1, 1, 8).

9TH ROW K0 (0, 0, 1, 8), (yfwd, K4, K2 tog tbl) 0 (0, 0, 1, 1) time/s, K3 (6, 2, 1, 1), * K2 tog, K4, yfwd, K5, yfwd, K4, K2 tog tbl, K1, rep from * to last 2 (5, 1, 7, 14) st/s, (K2 tog, K4, yfwd) 0 (0, 0, 1, 1) time/s, K2 (5, 1, 1, 8).

11TH ROW (K2, yfwd, K2 tog tbl, K3) 0 (0, 0, 0, 1) time/s, (K2 tog, yfwd, K1, K2 tog, K2, MI) 0 (0, 0, 1, 1) time/s, K3 (6, 2, 1, 1), * MI, K2, K2 tog tbl, K1, yfwd, K2 tog tbl, K3, K2 tog, yfwd, K1, K2 tog, K2, MI, K1, rep from * to last 2 (5, 1, 7, 14) st/s, (MI, K2, K2 tog tbl, K1, yfwd, K2 tog tbl) 0 (0, 0, 1, 1) time/s, (K3, K2 tog, yfwd) 0 (0, 0, 0, 1) time/s, K2 (5, 1, 0, 2).

13TH ROW (K3, yfwd, K2 tog tbl, K1, K2 tog) 0 (0, 0, 0, 1) time/s, (K2, K2 tog, K2, MI, K1) 0 (0, 0, 1, 1) time/s, K3 (6, 2, 1, 1),

* K1, MI, K2, K2 tog tbl, K1, yfwd, K2 tog tbl, K1, K2 tog, yfwd, K1, K2 tog, K2, MI, K2, rep from * to last 2 (5, 1, 7, 14) st/s, K2 (5, 1, 1, 1), (MI, K2, K2 tog tbl, K1) 0 (0, 0, 1, 1) time/s, (yfwd, K2 tog tbl, K1, K2 tog, yfwd) 0 (0, 0, 0, 1) time/s, K0 (0, 0, 1, 3).

15TH ROW (K2, K2 tog tbl, K1, yfwd, K3 tog, yfwd) 0 (0, 0, 0, 1) time/s, (K1, K2 tog, K2, MI) 0 (0, 0, 1, 1) time/s, K3 (6, 2, 3, 3), * K2, MI, K2, K2 tog tbl, K1, yfwd, K3 tog, yfwd, K1, K2 tog, K2, MI, K3, rep from * to last 2 (5, 1, 7, 14) st/s, (K2, MI, K2, K2 tog tbl) 0 (0, 0, 1, 1) time/s, (K1, yfwd, K3 tog, yfwd) 0 (0, 0, 0, 1) time/s, K2 (5, 1, 1, 4).

17TH ROW K0 (0, 0, 0, 7), (K2 tog, K2, MI, K2) 0 (0, 0, 1, 1) time/s, K3 (6, 2, 2, 2), * K3, MI, K2, K2 tog tbl, K3, K2 tog, K2, MI, K4, rep from * to last 2 (5, 1, 7, 14) st/s, (K3, MI, K2, K2 tog tbl) 0 (0, 0, 1, 1) time/s, K2 (5, 1, 0, 7).

19TH ROW (K1, MI, K2, K2 tog tbl, K1, K2 tog, K2 MI) 0 (0, 0, 0, 1) time/s, K3 (6, 2, 8, 5), * K4, MI, K2, K2 tog tbl, K1, K2 tog, K2, MI, K5, rep from * to last 2 (5, 1, 7, 14) st/s, K2 (5, 1, 7, 4), (MI, K2, K2 tog tbl, K1, K2 tog, K2, MI, K1) 0 (0, 0, 0, 1) time/s.

21ST ROW Knit.

23RD ROW [K2, K2 tog, (K1, yfwd) twice, K1 K2 tog] 0 (0, 0, 0, 1) time/s, K3 (6, 2, 8, 6), * K5, K2 tog, (K1, yfwd) twice, K1, K2 tog tbl, K6, rep from * to last 2 (5, 1, 7, 14) st/s, [K5, K2 tog, (K1, yfwd) twice, K1, K2 tog] 0 (0, 0, 0, 1) time/s, K2 (5, 1, 7, 2).

24TH ROW As 2nd row.

Rows 1 to 24 inclusive form patt.

Cont in patt until work measures 43 (47, 64, 65, 66) cm from beg, ending with a purl row.

Shape shoulders

Keeping patt correct, cast off 8 (9, 12, 13, 14) sts at beg of next 6 rows, then 9 (8, 11, 13, 16) sts at beg of foll 2 rows.

Leave rem 29 (31, 35, 37, 39) sts on a stitch holder.

Front

Work as given for Back until there are 22 (22, 24, 26, 28) rows less than Back to beg of shoulder shaping.

Shape neck

NEXT ROW Patt 40 (43, 56, 62, 69), turn.

** Keeping patt correct, dec one st at neck edge in alt rows until 33 (35, 47, 52, 58) sts rem.
Work 7 (5, 5, 5, 5) rows. **

Shape shoulder
Keeping patt correct, cast off 8 (9, 12, 13, 14) sts at beg of next and alt rows 3 times in all.
Work 1 row.
Cast off.
Slip next 15 (15, 17, 17, 17) sts at centre onto a stitch holder and leave. With right side facing, join yarn to rem sts and patt to end.
Work as given from ** to **.
Work 1 row.

Shape shoulder
Complete as for other shoulder shaping.

Sleeves
Using 3.25 mm needles and MC, cast on 45 (45, 55, 55, 55) sts.
Work for 7 (7, 8, 8, 8) cm in rib as for lower band of Back, ending with a 1st row.
NEXT ROW Rib 2 (2, 8, 8, 8), [inc in next st, rib 2 (2, 1, 1, 1) 14 (14, 20, 20, 20)] times, rib 1 (1, 7, 7, 7). 59 (59, 75, 75, 75) sts.
Change to 4 mm needles.
Work in patt as for 1st (1st, 3rd, 3rd, 3rd) size of Back, at same time inc one st at each end of 5th and foll 6th (4th, 6th, 4th, 4th) rows until there are 75 (73, 95, 81, 99) sts, then in foll 8th (6th, 8th, 6th, 6th) rows until there are 79 (89, 103, 107, 113) sts, working extra sts into patt.
Cont without shaping until side edge measures 33 (38, 43, 43, 43) cm from beg, ending with a purl row.

Shape top
Keeping patt correct, cast off 9 (10, 9, 9, 10) sts at beg of next 6 (6, 8, 8, 8) rows.
Cast off rem sts.

Neckband
Using back stitch, join shoulder seams.
With right side facing, using set of 3.25 mm needles and MC, beg at left shoulder seam and knit up 90 (90, 110, 110, 110) sts evenly around neck edge (including sts from stitch holders).

1ST ROUND * (K1 tbl, P1) twice, K1 tbl, P5, rep from * to end.
Rep 1st round until neckband measures 3 (3, 4, 4, 4) cm from beg.
Cast off loosely in rib.

To make up
Using Bullion Stitch and C2, C3 and C4, embroider 2 (2, 3, 3, 3) wattle across each shoulder on front. Using C1 and Satin Stitch, embroider leaves to wattle as pictured. Using C5, C6 and C7 and Satin and Stem Stitch, embroider 4 (4, 6, 6, 6) boronia across front as pictured. Using C8, C9, C10 and C11 and Turkey Rug Stitch, with C8 in centre, embroider 2 (2, 4, 4, 4) gum blossom across next section of front as pictured. Then for Adult only, embroider two wattle and leaves in centre of next section as pictured. Using back stitch, sew in sleeves placing centre of sleeves to shoulder seams. Join side and sleeve seams.

Shy Boronia

Two different designs feature embroidered boronia blossom detail. Adult's cardigan has a textured pattern and child's jumper features diamond cable and lace textured pattern

Measurements

To fit chest	cm	76:81	86:91	97:102	107:112
	in	30:32	34:36	38:40	42:44
Actual measurement	cm	109	120	129	140
Length to back neck	cm	58	61	63	65
Sleeve seam	cm	43	43	43	43

Materials

CLECKHEATON COUNTRY 8 PLY 50G BALLS

	MC	15	16	17	18
DMC TAPESTRY WOOL					
(7506)	C1	1	1	1	1
(7489)	C2	1	1	1	1
(7700)	C3	1	1	1	1

1 pr each 4 mm (No 8) and 3.25 mm (No 10) knitting needles or the required size to give correct tension. 9 (9, 10, 10) buttons. 2 stitch holders.

ADULT'S CARDIGAN

Back

Using 3.25 mm needles and MC, cast on 95 (103, 113, 121) sts.

1ST ROW P1, * K1 tbl, P1, rep from * to end.

2ND ROW K1, * P1 tbl, K1, rep from * to end.

Rep 1st and 2nd rows 16 times, then 1st row once.

36TH ROW Rib 14 (12, 17, 15), * inc in next st, rib 2, rep from * to last 12 (10, 15, 13) sts, rib 12 (10, 15, 13). 118 (130, 140, 152) sts.

Change to 4 mm needles.

1ST ROW K25 (31, 36, 42), (P2, K4, P2, K22) twice, P2, K4, P2, K25 (31, 36, 42).

2ND ROW P25 (31, 36, 42), (K2, P4, K2, P22) twice, K2, P4, K2, P25 (31, 36, 42).

3RD ROW K25 (31, 36, 42), (P2, ybk, sl1, K1, yfwd, K2, psso, P2, K22) 3 times, knit to end.

4TH ROW As 2nd row.

Rep last 4 rows until work measures 26 (28, 29, 31) cm from beg, working last row on wrong side.

Work from graph in st st and bobbles until work measures 32 (34, 35, 37) cm from beg, working last row on wrong side.

TENSION

Before commencing your garment it is essential to first check your tension. This garment has been designed at a tension of 22 sts to 10 cm over st st, using 4 mm needles.

ABBREVIATIONS

Make Bobble = (K1, P1, K1, P1) all in next st, pass 2nd, 3rd and 4th st over first to form a bobble.

Shape armholes
Keeping graph correct, cast off 3 (4, 5, 6) sts at beg of next 2 rows.
Dec one st at each end of every row 1 (7, 11, 17) time/s, then in foll alt rows until 80 (84, 88, 92) sts rem.
Cont without shaping until work measures 56 (59, 61, 63) cm from beg, working last row on wrong side.

Shape shoulders
Keeping patt correct, cast off 8 (8, 9, 10) sts at beg of next 4 rows, then 8 (9, 9, 9) sts at beg of foll 2 rows.
Cast off rem 32 (34, 34, 34) sts.

Right Front

Using 3.25 mm needles and MC, cast on 59 (63, 67, 71) sts.
Work 4 rows rib as for Back.
** **5TH ROW** (buttonhole row) Rib 6, yfwd,

K2 tog, rib to end.
Work 13 rows rib. **
Rep from ** to ** once, then 5th row once.
Work 2 rows rib.
36TH ROW Rib 8 (8, 8, 7), * inc in next st, rib 2, rep from * to last 18 (16, 17, 16) sts, rib 7 (5, 6, 5), leave rem 11 sts on a stitch holder for front band. 59 (65, 70, 76) sts.
Change to 4 mm needles.
1ST ROW K26, P2, K4, P2, K25 (31, 36, 42).
2ND ROW P25 (31, 36, 42), K2, P4, K2, P26.
3RD ROW K26, P2, ybk, sl1, K1, yfwd, K2, psso, P2, knit to end.
4TH ROW As 2nd row.
Rep these 4 rows until work measures 26 (28, 29, 31) cm from beg, working last row on wrong side.
Work from graph in st st and bobbles until work measures same length as back to underarm, working last row on right side.

● = Make Bobble
(see Abbreviations)
□ = st st

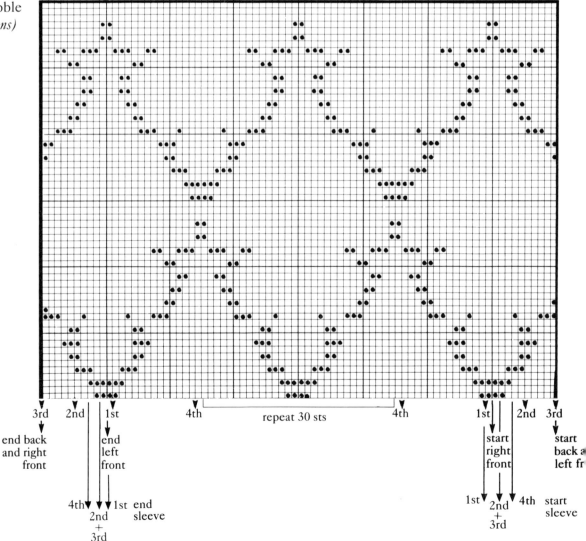

Shape armhole

Keeping graph correct, cast off 3 (4, 5, 6) sts at beg of next row.
Dec one st at armhole edge in every row 1 (7, 11, 17) time/s then in foll alt rows until 40 (42, 44, 46) sts rem.
Cont without shaping until work measures 48 (51, 53, 55) cm from beg, working last row on wrong side.

Shape neck

Keeping graph correct, cast off 6 (7, 7, 7) sts at beg of next row.
Dec one st at neck edge in alt rows until 24 (25, 27, 29) sts rem.
Cont without shaping until work measures same length as back to shoulder shaping, working last row on wrong side.

Shape shoulder

Cast off 8 (8, 9, 10) sts at beg of next row and foll alt row.
Work 1 row. Cast off.

Left Front

Using 3.25 mm needles and MC, cast on 59 (63, 67, 71) sts.
Work 35 rows rib as for Back.
36TH ROW Rib 11 and leave these sts on a stitch holder for front band, rib 7 (5, 6, 5), * inc in next st, rib 2, rep from * to last 8 (8, 8, 7) sts, rib 8 (8, 8, 7).
59 (65, 70, 76) sts.
Change to 4 mm needles.
1ST ROW K25 (31, 36, 42), P2, K4, P2, K26.
Complete to correspond with Right Front noting that patt and all shapings have been reversed.

Sleeves

Using 3.25 mm needles and MC, cast on 49 (51, 51, 53) sts.
Work 21 rows rib as for Back.
22ND ROW Rib 6 (6, 6, 5), * inc once in each of next 2 sts, rib 1, rep from * to last 7 (6, 6, 6) sts, inc in next st, rib 6 (5, 5, 5).
74 (78, 78, 82) sts.
Change to 4 mm needles.
1ST ROW K33 (35, 35, 37), P2, K4, P2, K33 (35, 35, 37).
2ND ROW P33 (35, 35, 37), K2, P4, K2, P33 (35, 35, 37).
Cont in patt as placed in last 2 rows as for

Back, inc one st at each end of 5th row, then in foll 6th rows until there are 92 (96, 96, 100) sts, working extra sts into patt.
Work 1 row.
Work from graph in st st and bobbles, inc one st at each end of 5th row, then in foll 6th rows until there are 106 (110, 110, 114) sts, working extra sts into patt.
Cont without shaping until side edge measures 43 cm from beg, working last row on wrong side.

Shape top

Keeping graph correct, cast off 3 (4, 4, 5) sts at beg of next 2 rows.
Dec one st at each end of every row until 48 (48, 48, 46) sts rem. Cast off.

Left Front Band

Using back stitch, join shoulder seams, matching patt carefully.
Using 3.25 mm needles and MC, rib across

sts from left front stitch holder and cont in rib until band fits (slightly stretched) to beg of neck shaping, working last row on wrong side.

Break off yarn. Leave sts on a stitch holder. Stitch band in place. Mark positions for 5 (5, 6, 6) more evenly spaced buttons above waist rib, allowing final button in Neckband.

Right Front Band

Work as for Left Front Band, working buttonholes as before to correspond with markers, working last row on wrong side. Do not break off yarn. Leave sts on a stitch holder. Stitch band in place.

Neckband

With right side facing, using 3.25 mm needles and MC, rib across sts from right front stitch holder, knit up 83 (87, 87, 87) sts evenly along neck edge, then rib across sts from left front stitch holder.
105 (109, 109, 109) sts.
Work 7 rows rib as for Back, beg with a 2nd row, working a buttonhole (as before) in 4th row.
Cast off loosely in rib.

To make up

Using back stitch, join side and sleeve seams. Sew in sleeves. Using DMC tapestry wool, embroider boronia on left and right fronts using Stem Stitch and Satin Stitch as pictured. Sew on buttons.

TENSION

Before commencing your garment it is essential to first check your tension. This garment has been designed at a tension of 22 sts to 10 cm over st st, using 4 mm needles.

CHILD'S JUMPER

Measurements

To fit chest	cm	61	66	71
	ins	24	26	28
Actual				
measurement *(approx)* cm		71	78	83
Length to back neck	cm	41	44	48
Sleeve seam	cm	26	31	36

Materials

CLECKHEATON COUNTRY 8 PLY 50G BALLS

		MC	7	8	9
DMC TAPESTRY WOOL					
(7506)	C1	1	1	1
(7700)	C2	1	1	1
(7489)	C3	1	1	1

1 pr each 4 mm (No 8), 3.25 mm (No 10) and 1 set of 3.25 mm (No 10) knitting needles or the required size to give correct tension. Cable needle. 2 stitch holders. Tapestry needle for embroidery.

Abbreviations

CR = Slip next st onto a cable needle and leave at back of work, K3, then K1 from cable needle.
CL = Slip next 3 sts onto a cable needle and leave at front of work, K1, then K3 from cable needle.
CRP = Slip next st onto a cable needle and leave at back of work, K3, then P1 from cable needle.
CLP = Slip next 3 sts onto a cable needle and leave at front of work, P1, then K3 from cable needle.

DIAMOND PANEL (worked over 24 sts)
1ST ROW P8, CR, CL, P8.
2ND AND ALT ROWS Knit all knit sts and purl all purl sts as they appear.
3RD ROW P7, CR, K2, CL, P7.
5TH ROW P6, CR, K4, CL, P6.
7TH ROW P5, CR, K6, CL, P5.
9TH ROW P4, CR, K8, CL, P4.
11TH ROW P3, CR, K10, CL, P3.
13TH ROW P2, CR, K12, CL, P2.
15TH ROW P1, CR, K14, CL, P1.
17TH ROW P1, CLP, K14, CRP, P1.
19TH ROW P2, CLP, K12, CRP, P2.
21ST ROW P3, CLP, K10, CRP, P3.
23RD ROW P4, CLP, K8, CRP, P4.

25TH ROW P5, CLP, K6, CRP, P5.
27TH ROW P6, CLP, K4, CRP, P6.
29TH ROW P7, CLP, K2, CRP, P7.
31ST ROW P8, CLP, CRP, P8.
32ND ROW As 2nd row.
Rows 1 to 32 inclusive form Diamond Panel.
LACE PANEL (worked over 11 sts)
1ST ROW K3, K2 tog, yfwd, K3, yfwd, sl 1, K1, psso, K1.
2ND AND ALT ROWS Purl.
3RD ROW K2, K2 tog, yfwd, K1, yfwd, sl 1, K1, psso, K2, yfwd, sl 1, K1, psso.
5TH ROW K1, K2 tog, yfwd, K3, yfwd, sl 1, K1, psso, K3.

7TH ROW K2 tog, yfwd, K2, K2 tog, yfwd, K1, yfwd, sl 1, K1, psso, K2.
8TH ROW Purl.
Rows 1 to 8 inclusive form Lace Panel.

Back

Using 3.25 mm needles and MC, cast on 74 (78, 86) sts.
1ST ROW K2, * P2, K2, rep from * to end.
2ND ROW P2, * K2, P2, rep from * to end.
Rep 1st and 2nd rows until work measures 6 (7, 8) cm from beg, ending with a 2nd row and inc 14 (16, 14) sts evenly across last row. 88 (94, 100) sts.
Change to 4 mm needles.
1ST ROW P0 (0, 2), K0 (1, 2), P0 (2, 2), * work 1st row of Lace Panel across next 11 sts, P2, K2, P2, work 1st row of Lace Panel across next 11 sts *, P2, K2, work 1st row of Diamond Panel across next 24 sts, K2, P2, rep from * to * once, P0 (2, 2), K0 (1, 2), P0 (0, 2).
2ND ROW K0 (0, 2), P0 (1, 2), K0 (2, 2), * work 2nd row of Lace Panel across next 11 sts, K2, P2, K2, work 2nd row of Lace Panel across next 11 sts *, K2, P2, work 2nd row of Diamond Panel across next 24 sts, P2, K2, rep from * to * once, K0 (2, 2), P0 (1, 2), K0 (0, 2).
3RD ROW As 1st row, working 3rd row of Lace and Diamond Panels.
Cont in patt as placed in last 3 rows (note that when each panel has been completed refer back to the 1st row of that panel patt. Panels will not end on same patt row) until work measures 40 (43, 47) cm from beg, working last row on wrong side.

Shape shoulders

Keeping patt correct, cast off 10 (10, 11) sts at beg of next 4 rows, then 9 (11, 12) sts at beg of foll 2 rows.
Leave rem 30 (32, 32) sts on a stitch holder.

Front

Work as given for Back until there are 22 (24, 24) rows less than Back to beg of shoulder shaping.

Shape neck

NEXT ROW Patt 36 (39, 42), turn.
** Keeping patt correct, dec one st at neck

edge in alt rows until 29 (31, 34) sts rem. Work 7 rows **.

Shape shoulder
Keeping patt correct, cast off 10 (10, 11) sts at beg of next row and foll alt row.
Work 1 row.
Cast off.
With right side facing, slip next 16 sts onto a stitch holder and leave. Join yarn to rem sts and patt to end.
Work as given from ** to **.
Work 1 row.

Shape shoulder
Complete as for other shoulder.

Sleeves

Using 3.25 mm needles and MC, cast on 38 (42, 46) sts.
Work for 5 (6, 6) cm in rib as for Back, ending with a 2nd row and inc 11 (13, 15) sts evenly across last row. 49 (55, 61) sts.
Change to 4 mm needles.
1ST ROW K0 (0, 2), P0 (1, 2), K0 (2, 2), P2 * work 1st row of Lace Panel across next 11 sts, P2, K2, P2, rep from * once (2 panels in all), work 1st row of Lace Panel across next 11 sts, P2, K0 (2, 2), P0 (1, 2), K0 (0, 2).
2ND ROW P0 (0, 2), K0 (1, 2), P0 (2, 2), K2, * work 2nd row of Lace Panel across next 11 sts, K2, P2, K2, rep from * once (2 panels in all), work 2nd row of Lace Panel across next 11 sts, K2, P0 (2, 2), K0 (1, 2), P0 (0, 2).
3RD ROW As 1st row, working 3rd row of Lace Panel.

4TH ROW As 2nd row, working 4th row of Lace Panel.
Cont in patt as placed in last 4 rows, inc one st at each end of next and foll 4th (6th, 6th) rows until there are 61 (65, 73) sts, then in foll 6th (8th, 8th) rows until there are 69 (73, 83) sts, working extra sts into patt.
Cont in patt without further shaping until side edge measures 26 (31, 36) cm from beg, working last row on wrong side.

Shape top
Keeping patt correct, cast off 7 (7, 8) sts at beg of next 8 rows.
Cast off rem sts.

Neckband

Using back stitch, join shoulder seams. With right side facing, using set of 3.25 mm needles and MC, knit up 88 (92, 96) sts evenly around neck edge (including sts from stitch holders).
1ST ROUND * K2, P2, rep from * to end. Rep 1st round until neckband measures 3 cm from beg.
Cast off loosely in rib.

To make up

Using C1, C2 and C3 and Satin and Stem Stitch, embroider boronia in centre of each diamond panel as pictured. Using C2 and Stem Stitch, embroider stem as pictured. Using back stitch, sew in sleeves placing centre of sleeves to shoulder seams. Join side and sleeve seams.

Delphinium

Adult's jumper worked in stocking stitch with delicately embroidered cable pattern bands and embroidered delphinium blossom detail

Measurements

To fit chest	cm	76:81	86:91	97:102
	in	30:32	34:36	38:40
Actual measurement	cm	101	111	122
Length to shoulder	cm	66	67	68
Sleeve seam	cm	43	43	43

Materials

CLECKHEATON COUNTRY 8 PLY 50G BALLS

	MC	14	15	16

DMC TAPESTRY WOOL

(7241)	C1	1	1	1
(7244)	C2	1	1	1
(7243)	C3	1	1	1
(7426)	C4	1	1	1
(7361)	C5	1	1	1

1 pr each 4 mm (No 8) and 3.25 mm (No 10) knitting needles or the required size to give correct tension. 2 stitch holders. Cable needle. Tapestry needle for embroidery.

Back

Using 3.25 mm needles and MC, cast on 113 (125, 137) sts.

1ST ROW (K1 tbl, P1) 0 (3, 6) times, P1, * K6, P2, (K1 tbl, P1) 3 times, P1 *, rep from * to * to last 7 (13, 19) sts, K6, P1, (P1, K1 tbl) 0 (3, 6) times.

2ND ROW (P1 tbl, K1) 0 (3, 6) times, K1, * P6, K2, (P1 tbl, K1) 3 times, K1 *, rep from * to * to last 7 (13, 19) sts, P6, K1, (K1, P1 tbl) 0 (3, 6) times.

3RD ROW (K1 tbl, P1) 0 (3, 6) times, P1, * CB, P2, (K1 tbl, P1) 3 times, P1 *, rep from * to * to last 7 (13, 19) sts, CB, P1, (P1, K1 tbl) 0 (3, 6) times.

4TH ROW As 2nd row.

Rep 1st and 2nd rows twice.

Last 8 rows form band patt.

Cont in band patt until work measures 8 cm from beg, working last row on wrong side.

Change to 4 mm needles. **

Cont in st st (1 row K, 1 row P) until work measures 63 (64, 65) cm from beg, ending with a purl row.

Shape back neck

NEXT ROW K47 (52, 57), turn.

Dec one st at neck edge in every row until 41 (46, 51) sts rem.

Work 1 row.

TENSION

Before commencing your garment it is essential to first check your tension. This garment has been designed at a tension of 22 sts to 10 cm over st st, using 4 mm needles.

ABBREVIATIONS

tbl = through back of loop.

CB = Slip next 3 sts onto a cable needle and leave at back of work, K3, then K3 from cable needle.

Shape shoulder

Cast off 10 (12, 13) sts at beg of next and foll alt rows 3 times in all. Work 1 row. Cast off.

With right side facing, slip next 19 (21, 23) sts onto a stitch holder and leave. Join yarn to rem sts and complete to correspond with other side of neck, reversing all shapings.

Front

Work as for Back to **.
Cont in st st until there are 26 (28, 28) rows less than Back to beg of shoulder shaping.

Shape neck

NEXT ROW K48 (54, 59), turn.
Dec one st at neck edge in foll alt rows until 41 (46, 51) sts rem.
Work 11 rows.

Shape shoulder

Complete as for Back.
With right side facing, slip next 17 (17, 19) sts onto a stitch holder and leave. Join yarn to rem sts and complete to correspond with other side of neck, reversing all shapings.

Sleeves

Using 3.25 mm needles and MC, cast on 50 sts.
Work for 8 cm in band patt as for 2nd size of Back, working last row on right side.
NEXT ROW Patt 4 (2, 0), * inc in next st, patt 1, rep from * to last 4 (2, 0) sts, patt 4 (2, 0). 71 (73, 75) sts.

Change to 4 mm needles.
Cont in st st, inc one st at each end of 5th row and foll 6th (6th, 4th) rows until there are 91 (101, 81) sts, then in foll 8th (8th, 6th) row/s until there are 99 (103, 107) sts. Cont without shaping until side edge measures 43 cm from beg, ending with a purl row.

Shape top

Cast off 10 (10, 11) sts at beg of next 6 rows, then 8 (10, 9) sts at beg of foll 2 rows. Cast off rem sts.

Neckband

Using back stitch, join right shoulder seam.

With right side facing, using 3.25 mm needles and MC, knit up 33 (33, 38) sts evenly along left side of front neck, knit across sts from front stitch holder inc (dec, inc) one st at end, knit up 33 (33, 38) sts evenly along right side of front neck, knit up 8 sts evenly along right side of back neck, knit across sts from back neck stitch holder inc 1 (1, 0) st at end, then knit up 8 sts evenly along left side of back neck. 120 (120, 135) sts.
1ST ROW Rep from * to * of 2nd row of Back.
2ND ROW Rep from * to * of 3rd row of Back. Cont in band patt as for Back as placed in last 2 rows, working from * to * of each patt row until neckband measures 4 cm from beg, working last row on wrong side, and dec 3 sts evenly across each cable on last row.
Cast off loosely.

To make up

Using C1, C2 and C3, embroider Satin Stitch delphinium flowers to left side of front. Work centre of flowers in Satin Stitch contrasting colours. Using C4 and C5, work Satin Stitch leaves at base of flower. Using C4, work a Stem Stitch stem to leaves as pictured. Using C3, embroider a French Knot in centre of each cable on all bands as pictured. Using back stitch, join left shoulder and side edge of neckband. Sew in sleeves placing centre of sleeves to shoulder seams. Join side and sleeve seams.

STITCH GLOSSARY

Knitting Stitch

Knitting Stitch embroidery is particularly effective on plain knitting (stocking stitch). Your garment can be quickly transformed by the addition of embroidered motifs to yoke or pockets. Children love to have an illustration from their favourite books transferred to a cardigan or jumper.

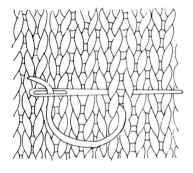

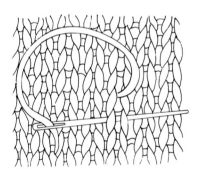

Use the same ply wool for embroidery as used in the garment. You could use a slightly thicker yarn if necessary, but a thinner yarn will not give a good result. Knitting Stitch is worked directly over each knitted stitch, with a contrasting colour to represent the same knitted stitch, as before. Each square on the graph represents one stitch. Insert the needle from back of work into the centre of the knitted stitch and draw through. *Insert needle from right to left, underneath the two loops of the same stitch one row above and draw through. Then insert needle back into original place where needle was first inserted, draw underneath the two loops still working from right to left, and out into the centre of the next stitch (thus completing one knitting stitch). Rep from * to end of graph pattern.

Odd numbered rows (knit rows) of pattern are worked from right to left and even numbered rows (purl rows) from left to right, until the motifs have been completed.

Stem Stitch

This is a widely used stitch as it is complementary to Satin Stitch and other filling stitches and is good for outlining and making curving lines. Working from left to right, pass the needle to the left under two or three threads of the fabric. Move along the line of the design to the right and make a second stitch to the left, picking up the same number of threads. The needle always emerges just above the previous stitch, giving the effect of a fine twisted cord.

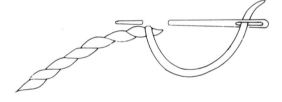

Back Stitch

This stitch is also frequently used in plain sewing. In embroidery, it is mainly used to make an outline, or as a base line for other decorative stitches. Working from right to left, bring the needle through to the right side of the fabric and make a small backward stitch. Bring the needle out the same number of threads to the left. Continue in this way, always returning to the end of the previous stitch.

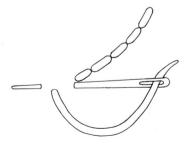

Satin Stitch

1. Working from left to right, bring the thread through on the lower edge of the shape and stitch into the opposite edge. Come out to the right of the first stitch, at a distance equal to the thickness of the thread being used, and stitch into the top edge in the same way.

2. Cover the entire surface of the shape. To achieve the smooth satin effect characteristic of this stitch, take care that the stitches are very even. To cover a large area, use an embroidery frame or ring, to ensure an even tension.

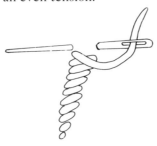

French Knot

Bring the thread through to the right side of the fabric. Take a tiny diagonal stitch, without pulling the needle through. Wind the thread around the needle two or three times and draw the needle through the knot. Stitch back into the fabric near the starting point, pulling the knot tight.

Bullion Stitch

Make a Back Stitch, the size of the Bullion Stitch required, and bring the needle point out where it first emerged, without pulling right through. Wind the thread round the needle point as many times as required. Holding the left thumb on the coiled thread, pull the needle through. Still holding the coiled thread, turn the needle back to where it was inserted and insert in the same place. Pull the needle through. Work stitches as illustrated to create wattle blossoms.

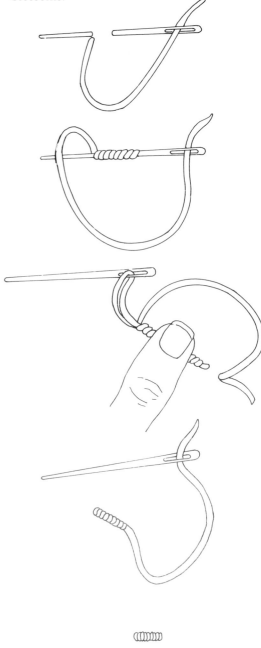

Turkey Rug Stitch

Work Back Stitch as illustrated but do not pull thread tight with each stitch. Instead, leave loops at front of work. Cut ends of loops, trimming evenly to achieve desired effect.

Chain Stitch (Cornelli Pattern)

Work crocheted chain until the desired length. Stitch lengths of chain onto garment using back stitch as illustrated. Follow graph or photograph for each garment as illustrated in individual patterns.

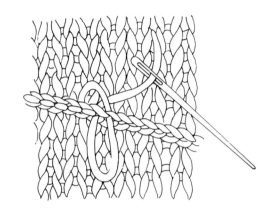

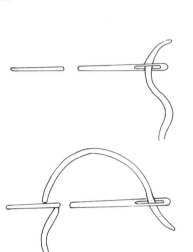

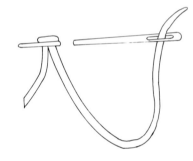

KNITTING NEEDLE SUGGESTED EQUIVALENT CHART

Canadian & UK Sizes	000	00	0	1	2	3	4	5	6	7	8	9	-	10	11	12	13
Metric Sizes	10	9	8	7 ½	7	6 ½	6	5 ½	5	4 ½	4	3 ¾	3 ½	3 ¼	3	2 ¾	2 ¼
US Sizes	15	13	11	-	-	10 ½	10	9	8	7	6	5	4	3	.	2	1

AMERICAN KNITTERS
PLEASE NOTE:
The American equivalents of Australian terminologies are as follows:

AUSTRALIAN	AMERICAN
yfwd	yarn over (yo)
yrn	yarn over (yo)
tension	gauge
cast off	bind off

May Gibbs — naturalist, psychologist and artist explorer has mapped out a world of her own and conquered it completely.

ADELAIDE ADVERTISER 1918

Tales of Snugglepot and Cuddlepie was combined with its two sequels, *Little Ragged Blossom* and *Little Obelia*, in 1940. Since then the *Complete Adventures of Snugglepot and Cuddlepie* has never been out of print and the magic of the May Gibbs characters still enchants children and adults today. Angus & Robertson Publishers produce a range of beautiful children's books, stationery items and craft titles featuring the ever popular May Gibbs characters.

Complete Adventures of Snugglepot and Cuddlepie (H/B)

Complete Adventures of Snugglepot and Cuddlepie (P/B)

May Gibbs Alphabet Book

Alphabet Frieze

The Story of Little Obelia

The Story of Ragged Blossom

The Story of Snugglepot and Cuddlepie

Tiny Story of Snugglepot and Cuddlepie

Wattle Babies

Boronia Babies

Flannel Flower Babies

Gum Blossom Babies

Gumnut Babies

May Gibbs Address Book

May Gibbs Baby Book

May Gibbs Birthday Book

MAY GIBBS AND VICKY KITANOV

Ten Little Gumnuts

Ten Little Gumnuts Frieze

Ten Little Gumnuts Miniature

A Gumnut's Year

PROJECT MANAGER:
Kate Tully

KNITTING CONSULTANT:
Kathy Jarvis, Cleckheaton

STYLIST:
Louise Owens

PHOTOGRAPHER:
Andrew Elton

MAKE-UP:
Julie Elton

FLOWERS:
Lisa Milasas

EMBROIDERY CONSULTANTS:
Neree Hartog (DMC), Alison Snepp

GARMENT FINISHERS:
Betty Callow, Maria Scherger

GARMENT KNITTERS:
Helen Cooper, Jennifer Smith, Kay Batt, Susan Howell,
Jennifer Legg, Freida Mouric, Lorraine Hessels, June
Mullis, Eileen McKoy, Vicki Baxter, June Martin,
Margaret Maltman, Nancy Williamson, Barbara Pritchard

The publishers would like to thank the following for their assistance:

MODELS CLOTHES WERE SUPPLIED BY
Just Jeans, stores throughout Australia and New Zealand,
Head Office (03)420 0200
Pumpkin, 35 Bay street, Double Bay 2028, (02)362 4362
Shoes & Sox, Shop 225/Westfield Chatswood, Victoria
Avenue, Chatswood 2067, (02)411 8840
Titbitz, 99 Devonshire Street, Surry Hills 2010,
(02)318 1474
2 Much, PO Box 1096, Strawberry Hills 2012, (02)310 3888

Make-up was supplied by Clarins.

A BAY BOOK PUBLICATION
An imprint of HarperCollinsPublishers

First published in Australia in 1993 by Bay Books

Bay Books, of
CollinsAngus&Robertson Publishers Pty Limited
A division of HarperCollins Publishers (Australia) Pty Limited
25 Ryde Road, Pymble NSW 2073, Australia

HarperCollinsPublishers (New Zealand) Limited
31 View Road, Glenfield, Auckland 10, New Zealand

HarperCollinsPublishers Limited
77-85 Fulham Palace Road, London W6 8JB, United Kingdom

National Library of Australia
Cataloguing-in-Publication data:

ISBN 1 86378 005 X

1. Knitting - Patterns. 2. Knitting - Australia - Patterns. 3. Sweaters - Australia. I. Gibbs,
May, 1877-1969.

746.92

Typeset in 10.5 Caslon
Printed by Griffin Press Pty Ltd, Netley, South Australia
76543
97 96 95 94 93